# MERCIFULLY

## ENJOYING FRUIT
IN YOUR LAND OF AFFLICTION

**GEORGE PANTAGES**

George Pantages Ministries

Copyright © 2013

Mercifully Afflicted

by George Pantages

Printed in the United States of America

ISBN 978-0-9827695-6-0

All rights reserved solely by the author. The author guarantees all contents are original and do not infringe upon the legal rights of any other person or work. No part of this book may be reproduced in any form without the permission of the author.

Unless stated otherwise, all Scripture references come from the NKJV translation of the Bible, copyright © 2006 Thomas Nelson.

KJV. Copyright © 2006 by Thomas Nelson.

George Pantages Ministries

## TABLE OF CONTENTS

Chapter 1
**Mercifully Afflicted** ……………………………… 9

Chapter 2
**Hidden Jewels**……………………………….. 23

Chapter 3
**Battle Scars**………………………………………… 37

Chapter 4
**The Unknown Soldier**………………………….. 51

Chapter 5
**In the Eye of the Beholder**…………………….. 65

Chapter 6
**Enjoying Fruit in Your Land of Affliction**………. 79

Chapter 7
**The Tenderness of a Woman**………………….. 93

Chapter 8
**He Heard my Cry**……………………………….. 107

Chapter 9
**In the Palm of His Hand**……………………….. 121

Chapter 10
**Nevertheless, God Will Make a Way**……………… 135

# DEDICATION

I would like to dedicate this book to two great men of God, ones the Lord had chosen to help me further my ministry when we moved to Texas:

John Burnett-It took a genuine move of God in your life to change your mind about my ministry and I'm glad it happened. Not because you became such a great influence opening doors for me in Spanish ministries, but the fact that with that change I gained a great friend. I admire your zeal for God and how your love for others truly exemplifies the love of Christ. What has made an even greater impact on my life is your integrity. Thank you for being the great example you have been but even more so I am grateful we have become colleagues with a similar vision for the lost. Again, thank you my friend, thank you!

Leon Suggett-When my type as you talk program tried to spell your full name it came out Leon "said it." How in the world did it know? From the first day we met up until now you have talked my ears off and then some. But the thing that I admire of you the most is that when you talk, it's always about the things of the Lord. When you initially were enamored with my ministry and promised to hook me up with other pastors in the organization, I wasn't sure if I were to take you serious or not. You sure held up your end of the bargain when you connected me with Jeff Arnold and with that being said I will never doubt your word again. In all seriousness, thank you for all the stories, testimonies, and encouragement you have given me, they are priceless!

## APPRECIATION

I would like to take the time to appreciate the following people for their contribution on the publication of this book:

Michelle Levigne - Editor

Ricardo Canchola Yáñez – Book Cover Design

Your professionalism and expertise rang true throughout the entire process, making my writing a whole lot better than it really is.

## INTRODUCTION

Afflictions and their purpose have changed immensely. The Old Testament view of this period of suffering was one where God was seeking retribution for the sins of His people. Man would not be able to escape the heavy hand of God thus he had to pay for his sin. Another train of thought was the fact that the Lord used afflictions as a form of discipline. They were lessons taught to help man save himself from pride and presumption (Job 33:14-30). With the law doing its part in condemning just about everything done by Israel, hope for mankind in the eyes of God's people had dwindled almost to nothing.

Sadly to say amongst many Christians today, not much has changed. A God that is constantly judging and condemning is the conception a number of saved people have when they think about their God. Being paralyzed and somewhat stunted in their spiritual growth, they stumble in the dark never being able to find the perfect will of God.

As New Testament doctrine began to surface after the death of Christ, a great paradigm shift followed as well. A new way of seeing affliction was emphasized in God's word, so much so that it has taken such a long time for us as Christians today to see the positives in our afflictions.

This book was written with the intent and purpose of helping today's Christian make that paradigm shift as well. It is time to leave the old behind and allow the new to take its place. *And no one puts new wine into old wineskins; or else the new wine bursts the wineskins, the wine is spilled, and the wineskins are ruined. But new wine must be put into new wineskins.* (Mark 2:22)

God is willing to do a "new thing" in our lives if through the furnace of affliction we can be purified. His new wine, the fullness of His Spirit (Ephesians 5:18) must be able to utilize a vessel that will not only be long-lasting but one that would bring honor to Him. If enduring afflictions will have that kind of results, here I am Lord use me!

# CHAPTER 1

## Mercifully Afflicted

*For He says to Moses, "I will have mercy on whomever I will have mercy, and I will have compassion on whomever I will have compassion."*
(Romans 9:15)

While I was ministering one day, out of the corner of my eye I peeked over to look at the next person in line. At first glance, the young lady nervously waiting for her turn did not look physically hurt in any way, shape, or form. I was curious to see what her petition would be when she had the chance. She woefully blurted out that although married for two-and-a-half years, she still could not get pregnant.

"All I want from the Lord is a healthy baby," she said. As I gazed upon her, waiting for what type of message I should give her from the Lord, it suddenly came to mind. I told her this emphatically, "The Lord indeed will bless you with a little girl and she will be born in the month of April."

As the words were coming out of my mouth, you could see her countenance change. With glee she began to repeat over and over, "Oh, God, I can't believe it, I am going to have a baby." As soon as the opportunity presented itself, she began to publicize it to anyone and everyone within earshot.

It was at this time that a great affliction would be an unwanted companion, for the next several years. Of course, when the prophecy was made public, all of us assumed that the month of April meant April of the following year. The way it turned out was not what God had in mind. Later that year when she did not get pregnant, the doubts began to surface. April of the next year rolled around and there was no sign of a newborn. Initially, she tried to play it off as no big deal. As time wore on, the mental anguish began to increase. The first to be criticized for the unfulfilled prophecy was she herself.

"I know what happened, I just didn't have enough faith," she said.

As time continued to produce the same results, believing she was at fault became offensive. The emotional beatings she had to endure were more than she could stomach. Surely the blame for this entire mess could be placed elsewhere, but who would that be? These were dark days for her, both literally and spiritually, and there did not appear to be a let up or a way out.

### An About-Face Occurs

It is difficult at times, trying to figure out how, where, and when a turnaround comes about in our lives. Hope springs eternal, and I believe that it is hope that sustains us in times that just don't make any sense. As we search the Scriptures for relief, we find ones such as this that bring our hope up to a different level.

> *I know that the LORD will maintain the cause of the afflicted, and justice for the poor. Surely the*

*righteous shall give thanks to Your name; The upright shall dwell in Your presence.*
*(Psalms 140:12-13)*

With that in mind, a sudden about-face took place. Her "woe is me" attitude was replaced by a worshiping spirit. Although she didn't understand it and could not explain it, if the Lord chose a life without children for her, then that would be acceptable. She would no longer mope or complain about her dilemma, she would take the high road and became a worshiper like none other. She would continually give thanks and make sure that dwelling in His presence would become her passion.

*I will bless the LORD at all times; His praise shall continually be in my mouth. My soul shall make its boast in the LORD; The humble shall hear of it and be glad. Oh, magnify the LORD with me, and let us exalt His name together.* *(Psalms 34:1-3)*

Her new mindset did wonders for her marriage. Not only did her relationship with God continue to ripen, so did her relationship with her husband. The love and affection she felt for these two people in her life were enough to help her feel fulfilled and in want of nothing. By this time, the memory of the prophecy was nothing more than a bad joke. It had been filed away in the back of her mind as something that could not be explained. It was only then, when she had completely dismissed the idea of having children that the unexpected happened.

### The Unexpected Happened

"You're pregnant and you're going to have a baby, congratulations," said the doctor.

In apparent shock, she did not know how to respond. "Should I yell, scream, do a little dance?" she said to herself. "This cannot be happening. I have waited eight years and pretty much given up hope, and it is happening now? Now, right now? It's just so hard to believe." As the thought of being pregnant was starting to sink in, there was another question that needed to be settled. "I wonder if it's going to be a girl, just like the man of God said. I better not get my hopes up; it's good enough that I am going to have a baby."

A few months later, the sonogram would confirm the prophecy. "You're going to have a little girl," said the doctor. Chills began to make their way up and down her spine, making her heart do flip-flops.

The year of her pregnancy was 2011, approximately six years after the original prophecy. I had not returned to that part of the country since then, and when I initially found out she did not have the baby the following April, I wasn't sure what to expect if she ever wanted to talk. I received a message on Facebook from a person I did not recognize. She wrote: *Praise the Lord Bro. Pantages! When you came to Seattle you prophesied and said that my baby was going to be born in April and finally the miracle has come. She will be born this April (2012). Her name will be Alexis Eliana Sandoval. We have decided to name her Eliana as a middle name because it means God has responded!*

If the testimony would have ended there the way I had originally thought, it would have been one of the greatest miracles God had produced in my ministry. The problem arose when the enemy was not willing to sit back and let the glory of God manifest itself without any opposition. It was then his best scare tactic was put into play. Through the doctor, he intimidated her to induce labor before the due date. The baby up to that point was completely healthy and was in no danger of losing its life. That being said, her problems with high blood pressure and her inexperience in trusting God for great things caused her to make a decision that would change the prophecy altogether. Per her doctor's advice, to be on the safe side, labor was induced and the baby was born on February 27.

### The Truth about Personal Prophecy

For those of you reading this without much experience in dealing with personal prophecy, let me take a little bit of time to shed some light. First of all, a personal prophecy (which this was) is a prophecy with conditions. That means God is willing to bring this to pass if, and only if, our part is done as well. If there is any failure to complete the instructions as given, then the prophecy will either fail or be changed.[1] In this case, the prophecy changed because the mother decided to play it safe. There was no real harm done, the baby was born, it was a little girl, and both parents were completely satisfied with the results. Personal prophecy is always a prophecy for a specific person for a specific situation for a specific time. If all of those things fall into place, then the prophecy will come to pass as prophesied.

### Was This Really Necessary?

Evidently the waiting period was entirely worth it, but was the affliction that accompanied it really necessary? Why did she have to wait so long? The sleepless nights, the nervous stomach, the uncertainty growing with each and every passing day, the ridicule she received when it did not come to pass. Was it really mandatory to receive her blessing? What about the fact that she actually received an answer to her petition when countless others found themselves still waiting for their answer? What was so special about her and her situation that separated it from the rest of the crowd? Of all the questions being asked today, the last one is the simplest to answer.

> *For He says to Moses, "I will have mercy on whomever I will have mercy, and I will have compassion on whomever I will have compassion."*
> (Romans 9:15)

The Lord is sovereign in all that He does. How and why He chooses the way He chooses can never be figured out. The only conclusion we can come to is that He always has our best interests in mind. His mercy always demonstrates an act of favor or compassion. That being said, one must realize that it is always selective, not deserved. We can find ourselves going down a slippery slope when we assume, as His children, He is obligated to give us what we are asking. Although His mercy has far-reaching effects, extending to those who have broken His law as well as those who are suffering due to circumstances beyond their control, the bottom line is that He makes the final decision. He is a faithful God, true to His word, and we can always depend on Him.

> *Through the LORD's mercies we are not consumed, because His compassions fail not. They are new every morning; Great is Your faithfulness.*
> (Lamentations 3:22-23)

### Dealing with Afflictions

Moreover, dealing with afflictions is another matter. Afflictions are nothing more than any condition or problem that produces suffering or pain, both physical and/or mental. It also means to distress so severely as to cause persistent anguish, to injure by humbling.[2] If we put it in biblical terms, we find out that God allows afflictions to come into our lives for two reasons. The first one is somewhat pessimistic in that it represents God's judgment (Romans 2:9). When we have crossed the line outside of the boundaries of God's laws, afflictions of judgment play a part in reconciling us to God. This is the mindset that the church has embraced since its inception, and it has hindered God's positive way of afflicting His people. For generations, condemnation and judgment were such an integral part of serving God that focusing on the negative took precedent. The Lord was perceived as a heavy taskmaster, and if you were not perfect, pending judgment was just around the corner. But God also uses afflictions to purify the believer as he identifies with Christ[3] (Romans 5:3-5). This ongoing cleansing is essential to chip away at our natural man. After the Garden of Eden fiasco, man had to start from square one to get back into God's good graces. Afflictions at various times in our lives will accomplish that task.

As we try to link together affliction with mercy, it would appear to be a recipe for disaster. Whereas with magnets positives or negatives repel each other, in this situation it's more like the results we obtain when opposites attract. You know what I mean. It's like when the quiet, shy young man is star-struck by that loud, out-of-control young lady. If the strengths of both can be melded together, the relationship will work. Where mercy and affliction are concerned, if the strengths of both characteristics can be fused together, they will lead us closer to the image of Christ. This celestial union becomes a "Merciful Affliction." Its full impact can be found in the calming of the storms in life, repairing that broken heart, restoring damaged relationships, and resurrecting ministries that had been left for dead. With a better handle on what the two can do together, let's take a biblical example of what I have described.

### A Classic Study

The Old Testament story of Leah is a classic study in true love. Her life from the get-go was a constant uphill battle. As a woman living in those times, she was considered a second class citizen. Her physical affliction as an unattractive woman only made matters worse. Her name said it all. The name Leah means: tires one out, wild cow.[4] When Leah came into the life of her husband Jacob (an expert in the art of conniving), he had to concede that he had met his match in this skillful craft. She was a deceiver par excellence and she honestly lived up to her name. Jacob would later learn firsthand how her rants and raves could be ever so tiring. When situations arose to upset her, that "wild cow" nature reared its ugly head, releasing unrestrained emotions, causing irreparable damage. There was no sense of wrongdoing when she and her father finagled the laws of the land to get her married to Jacob. It was commonly understood that most marriages of that time in that part of the world were prearranged anyway. In her mind, he would just have to learn to love her, just like all of the other marriages that were arranged for reasons other than love. The obstacle she did not take into consideration was that Jacob was madly in love with her younger sister, Rachel. And why not? She was drop-dead gorgeous, with an hourglass figure on steroids that would not quit, and she was willing to marry Jacob.

### Misinterpreting God's Mercy

Fighting for his love would be her only recourse to win him over, and she didn't have a problem with that because her wild nature would be to her advantage. It was at this point in her life that the afflictions haunting her became emotional. She, of all people, misinterpreted the mercy God was trying to bestow upon her. The Lord had seen that she was unloved and tried to rectify it.

> *When the LORD saw that Leah was unloved, He opened her womb; but Rachel was barren So Leah conceived and bore a son, and she called his name Reuben; for she said, "The LORD has surely looked on my affliction. Now therefore, my husband will love me."* (Genesis 29:31,32)

She had reasoned within herself that bearing children would be the key to unlocking the door of Jacob's heart. She was totally convinced that her years of being unloved were finally coming to an end. She would decisively have the upper hand over her more favored sister, Rachel, and there was nothing she could do about it. Sad to say, it wasn't enough. The ironclad grip Rachel had on Jacob's love was impossible to loosen. This realization only added fuel to the fire. The emotional disdain for Rachel that was already out of control continued to run roughshod.

### *A Great Turnaround Occurs*

Something interesting occurred at the birth of her fourth son, Judah. This about-face that would come out of nowhere was completely unexpected. It had to be a God thing. Only the Lord could produce such a drastic change in a person in so little time. The focus of her life seemed to be altered in such a way that she no longer dwelt on what she could not control (i.e., Jacob's love), but her attention would now be centered on praising God. Her affliction now had purpose. Like the psalmist David, she could joyfully say:

> *Before I was afflicted I went astray, but now I keep Your word. You are good, and do good; Teach me Your statutes.* (Psalms 119:67-68)

The afflictions of her life had completely dominated her thinking, 24/7. That in and of itself helped her come to the realization that she was on the wrong path in life. Whether Jacob came to his senses to love her for whom she was or not, it would no longer consume her every waking moment. Praising God and lifting up the name of Jehovah would now become her lifelong passion.

Her unlikely turnaround impressed God, as praising Him will always do. We were created to praise God, and it becomes even more impressive to Him when our praise comes at a time of suffering that leaves an ugly taste in our mouths.

> *Whoever offers praise glorifies Me; and to him who orders his conduct aright I will show the salvation of God."* (Psalms 50:23)

When our praise glorifies God, His attributes become a part of us and our conduct changes. It does not matter what walk of life you come from. God will put it in order as your praises magnify Him. A whole new world of blessing is now at our fingertips because of our willingness to offer a sacrifice of praise. The wholesale changes that become part of our DNA make us more godlike, conformed to His image.

Leah's love for people, in essence, became godlike. Her unconditional love, in spite of herself, began to radiate as the Lord's did here on earth as He ministered unto the needy. With each and every passing day, it was easy to see that Leah was living a completely different life. It is amazing what godlike characteristics in a person can do for someone who is not physically appealing to the eye. It won't necessarily make you eye candy; nevertheless, it will cause people to wonder what it is about you that draws them. It was this unforeseen transformation that ultimately caught Jacob's eye, and captured his heart and love as well.

My words of speculation appear to be written with great latitude, because there is no Scripture that will confirm that train of thought. Before I prove through history that my words are on target, let me say this about the effect of Leah's life on future generations.

From history, we find that if we charted Leah's bloodline, it would take us directly to the birth of Jesus Christ. That clearly meant she was family, and we all know that family pass on to their relatives not only physical traits, but character traits as well. I believe that the same grit, tenacity, and drive demonstrated through the afflictions of her life were the same traits Jesus used to complete His assignment at Calvary. He didn't quit because she didn't quit. What a legacy she passed on. Coming off of the cross was not even an option, because He had a great example to follow in the life of Leah. She loved Jacob even when she knew that that same love would not be returned. In like fashion, Jesus was willing to give His life on the cross, whether anyone would accept His gift or not. His affliction would run its course with nary an opposition; He would silently take it like a man.

> *He was oppressed and He was afflicted, Yet He opened not His mouth; He was led as a lamb to the slaughter, and as a sheep before its shearers is silent, So He opened not His mouth.* (Isaiah 53:7)

Rachel would have never had the stubbornness, resolve, or persistence to complete such a task. Her legacy passed on to future generations would have been completely different than that of her older, less talented sister. Leah truly was a diamond in the rough. With coarse edges on every side, the grinding and polishing of her various afflictions finally brought something beautiful to the surface.

### Connecting the Dots

Now let me connect the dots to let you in on how I came to the conclusion Leah was eventually loved by Jacob. Scripturally, we really don't know what happened in their marriage from the time of her turnaround until her death. It was at her death that the speculation ended and we have visual proof of the love Jacob had for his neglected wife. If we were to go to the Middle East today and look in the cave of Machpelah, we would find the great patriarchs of Israel buried there. We would find Abraham and his wife, Sarah. Next to them, Isaac and Rebekah are buried. This is also the final resting place for Jacob and his wife...? It was Leah, of course, and not Rachel. For all of the physical and emotional afflictions she had to cope with, her reward, this final resting place far outweighed the demoralizing afflictions she had to endure. Reading the Apostle Paul's words we find in Romans helps us to believe that he felt the same way.

> *For I consider that the sufferings of this present time are not worthy to be compared with the glory which shall be revealed in us* (Romans 8:18)

As wonderfully as Leah's life ended, it really was just the beginning of a better life. It did not matter to her that it didn't happen while she was alive. The fact of the matter was, she, not Rachel, was buried next to her husband. It was the highest honor a woman could receive in those times.

Just think, if it had not been for the afflictions in her life, she would've never been exposed to the mercy of God. It was through His merciful afflictions, at the center of it all, that she found a genuine long-lasting relationship with God. Isn't this the true meaning of life? Being able to find God, establish a relationship with Him, and receive all the benefits of serving the one and true God is on everyone's wish list.

### *His Mercy is Always Greater Than Our Afflictions*

As we re-examine the life of the young mother-to-be at the outset of this chapter, it is easy to see the similarities in her life and in that of Leah. Fighting afflictions, whether physical or emotional, put them together on common ground. The pain a woman must endure during childbirth is a unique one only known to womankind. A man cannot even compare it to the most painful situation that he would ever have to tolerate. The physical demands are one thing, quite grueling and utterly exhausting. That does not even take into consideration the mental fatigue a woman must endure during childbirth. It is so strenuous on both ends that I have heard the strongest of women blurt out shamefully, "I'll never do this again." But something amazing takes place when the baby is placed for the first time in mama's bosom. All of the pain, agony, and torture experienced are but a distant memory because the fruit of her labor far outweighs the pain. When the trials and severe afflictions come to inflict their pain, we must take on the same attitude as these childrearing mothers. Yes, the afflictions will take their toll in every which way they can, but the mercy of God being invoked will be far greater than what we must suffer.

> *Now no chastening seems to be joyful for the present, but painful; nevertheless, afterward it yields the peaceable fruit of righteousness to those who have been trained by it.* (Hebrews 12:11)

My Hispanic upbringing tells me that this scripture is a very discouraging one. The Spanish word translated for chastening is punishing. We all know that training is painful, yet very needful to advance in whatever area we are trying to improve. To have to accept that we are being punished for attempting to better ourselves just doesn't make any sense. It is in reality counterproductive. Instead of encouraging us to better develop and hone our skills in the things of the Lord, it makes us wary to even attempt such an undesirable undertaking. It is difficult enough to complete our training without every once in a while looking over our shoulder to see if a heavy-handed God is there, waiting to deal with us harshly.

On the other hand, with a positive outlook, we can maneuver our way through these spiritual afflictions in a manner that will be pleasing unto our Master. Nevertheless, it will be a painful experience, one that cannot be avoided. Yet, when it is all over, like that woman after childbirth, we will be willing to do it again. The peaceable fruit of righteousness will help us to see that our training was worth it and that the blessings we originally believed were hidden *from* us are in actuality hidden *for* us. His mercy will always continue to be greater than our afflictions. It is a total sacrifice of praise from us that God needs to see to unleash His glory. Is that all that you are lacking today? Remember, grateful praise will always catch His attention, and with that praise bring your afflictions to rest.

# CHAPTER 2
## Hidden Jewels

*Behold, I have refined you, but not as silver; I have tested you in the furnace of affliction. For My own sake, for My own sake, I will do it; For how should My name be profaned? And I will not give My glory to another.* (Isaiah 48:10-11)

As the phrase "furnace of affliction" rolls off your tongue, it is very difficult to believe that there is anything constructive about this experience. Of course this furnace, like all others, is a place for refining. Figuratively speaking, its purpose is to free one from moral imperfections. The process is similar to the refining of metals with either extreme heat, and/or fire. If refining is completely successful, the results will present a clear and unmistakable impression. It is always the goal in spiritual refining to produce a product (i.e., a child of God) that will look and act pretty much like the Lord Jesus Christ. An added benefit to this process comes when subtleties are enhanced. In terms of the Christian life, praise, worship, and our relationships with God become skillful and expert. To obtain best results, the affliction must run its course. Pain, suffering, and loss must not short-circuit the purifying process.

If you honestly take the time to delve into the lives of those in the Lord who have been successful, a common thread will be found. No matter who you choose, they will have suffered afflictions, not only more severely, but more in number as well. In humbling themselves time and time again, they have allowed the refining process to chip away at those needless characteristics hindering God from bringing them to a place of perfection. Do they shine more brightly than other children of God? Undoubtedly so, their brilliance far exceeds that of others. But there is something else that must be taken into account, and that is the price they have paid to get there far exceeds that of others as well.

### Judah in the Furnace of Affliction

In the Scripture above, Judah had been refined in the furnace of affliction. Notice how the Lord went out of His way to help them see the process was not the same as when silver was refined. Silver, in biblical types and figures, has always dealt with purity. His people knew they were not ready to dedicate themselves totally onto God because the cost would have been too high. In the eyes of the Lord, their half in/half out worship would not be acceptable. Hence, the refining process was held back just enough to bring repentance to His wayward children. Why would God even bother to deal with a bunch that could not decide where their allegiances were? An even greater sin amongst the Babylonians was taking place. God's name was being profaned. Because of Judah's unfaithfulness, they were placed under Babylonian captivity, which in turn gave the Babylonians an opportunity to mock their God. The glory that should have been reserved for Jehovah was being placed in the hands of lesser gods. If there is one thing God will not tolerate, it is giving His glory to another. These "Merciful Afflictions" were established for one reason and one reason only. Judah needed to get down on their knees and repent of their sins by calling on His name. This ultimately would allow Him to unleash His glory and place it back where it belonged.

The similarities between Judah's lackadaisical serving of their God and that of the Church of today are simply eerie. A lukewarm spirit dominating the Church of today is unacceptable, because including the world in the Christian life will not be satisfactory in the eyes of God.

> *"I know your works, that you are neither cold nor hot. I could wish you were cold or hot. So then, because you are lukewarm, and neither cold nor hot, I will vomit you out of My mouth. Because you say, 'I am rich, have become wealthy, and have need of nothing' — and do not know that you are wretched, miserable, poor, blind, and naked — I counsel you to buy from Me gold refined in the fire, that you may be rich; and white garments, that you may be clothed, that the shame of your nakedness may not be revealed; and anoint your eyes with eye salve, that you may see.* (Revelation 3:15-19)

You cannot equate wealth and prosperity with acceptance in the kingdom of God. The church of Laodicea, in the eyes of outsiders, was rich and in need of nothing. It was a spiritual giant in its heyday. But in the eyes of God, the church of Laodicea was wretched, miserable, poor, blind, and naked. How could there be such a great disparity between what others saw and what God saw? If how we live is going to stand the test of time once it comes out of the furnace of affliction, the refining process will tell the true story. The remaining qualities refined to perfection will be those that will please the Lord.

> *that you may walk worthy of the Lord, fully pleasing Him, being fruitful in every good work and increasing in the knowledge of God; strengthened with all might, according to His glorious power, for all patience and longsuffering with joy;*
> 
> (Colossians 1:10-11)

### Hidden Jewels

If the furnace of affliction is so pertinent in the kingdom of God today, we must also mention the hidden jewels (we His children) that are discovered coming out of the fire. These jewels can be formed and perfected only through various afflictions, because it is God's way of separating the dross from the valuable. The process of finding these jewels is one that needs time. When we produce precious jewels, even in the world, it must take time. Of course, the refining process always begins by grace, and by grace salvation is secured. We are all then placed in the Kingdom of God in a great house where the sifting of the Saints begins.

> *But in a great house there are not only vessels of gold and silver, but also of wood and clay, some for honor and some for dishonor.* (2 Timothy 2:20)

The opportunity to succeed is given equally to us all. It is our choice whether we become vessels of honor or continue to dishonor Him in our lives. The furnace of affliction will always determine the outcome. We must come to understand that moving from wood and clay to gold and silver is not out of the question. Yes, we may have entered into the kingdom of God with not much to offer, but the furnace of affliction will not only free us from moral imperfections, it will also perfect our gifting that we might become a vessel of honor to Him. As a child of God, it is our right to pursue this with zeal and enthusiasm that cannot be quenched. Look what the apostle Paul said to the Ephesians concerning this subject:

> *But God, who is rich in mercy, because of His great love with which He loved us, even when we were dead in trespasses, made us alive together with Christ (by grace you have been saved), and raised us up together, and made us sit together in the heavenly places in Christ Jesus, that in the ages to come He might show the exceeding riches of His grace in His kindness toward us in Christ Jesus. For by grace you have been saved through faith, and that not of yourselves; it is the gift of God, not of works, lest anyone should boast. For we are His workmanship, created in Christ Jesus for good works, which God prepared beforehand that we should walk in them.* (Ephesians 2:4-10)

There's that word mercy again. It is at the root of His love, coupled with grace, to put on display His exceeding riches. We have been made to sit together in heavenly places in Christ Jesus, which gives us a unique vantage point in our lives. With Him sitting by our side, above all the distractions, all of a sudden the difficulties of life become manageable. We can see more clearly, and with that clarity take into consideration the big picture in our lives. We will then find ourselves with the ability to accomplish more and to accomplish it more skillfully. Here is the kicker. Because we are His workmanship and God doesn't create junk, we can have confidence in His word that we have been created in Christ Jesus for good works. It really boils down to two things. First, you must believe that the promise applies to your individual life. You cannot discount God's grace by saying you do not measure up, because that would be a slap in the face to the Master. Second, if you can handle the fire, you will not only shine brightly, but your life will bring honor and glory to God as well. There is enough grace for anyone and everyone who will let the furnace of affliction complete its refining work.

### Hidden Jewels in the Old Testament

Throughout history, God has always had hidden jewels. As we look to the Old Testament again, we can find at this particular point of Judah's history God's people were somewhat backslidden. Judah was spiritually in shambles because there was no leadership from King Ahaziah. When Jehu murdered the king, things went from bad to worse. His mother, Athaliah, took advantage of the chaos and proclaimed herself Queen. She was an idolatrous, Baal-worshiping, wicked woman whose first order of business was to kill all the male descendants of the throne. In other words, she had her grandchildren murdered. What kind of woman in the role of grandmother could assassinate her grandchildren at the drop of a hat? This was the type of woman Judah had to deal with from the get-go.   During the establishment of this new regime, her youngest grandson, about a year old at the time, was hidden from her. For the next six years, Joash was hidden in the safest place anyone could be hidden. At that time, no one would ever think to look in the Temple because Athaliah was a Baal worshiper, and she would not be caught dead in God's temple, so it was completely safe.

The fact that God chose a baby to deliver Judah from its wicked ways was somewhat puzzling, yet the reasoning was quite solid. Joash was young enough to have escaped his father's delusional philosophy of how the kingdom would worship God. By being trained in the ways of Jehovah daily in the Temple, it would guarantee that when the time arose for him to take his rightful place on the throne, he would bring peace to the land.

> This Book of the Law shall not depart from your mouth, but you shall meditate in it day and night, that you may observe to do according to all that is written in it. For then you will make your way prosperous, and then you will have good success.
> (Joshua 1:8)

His instruction began with nonstop attention, knowing that the word of God hidden in his heart would have a profound effect on how he would rule Judah. Six years later, he was still somewhat wet behind the ears when the call to the throne came. He was way too young and way too inexperienced to be an effective ruler, but being that it was God's timing, that in and of itself then made it the right time.

If there ever was a reason why God chooses ill-prepared and inexperienced people, it is this. It boils down to simple trust. The afflictions of anxiety and uneasiness are placed there to make you dependent on God. Then when the timing is right, it doesn't matter what the circumstances are, nothing and no one will be able to stop you. When all is said and done, those who have been watching will be amazed by your accomplishments. They will have to admit, coming to the conclusion that, "it had to be God." The glory will then go to the right place, that being glory to God.

When Joash came out of hiding, the boy king came out like gangbusters. Without lifting a finger, Jehoiada, the Temple priest, helped him to restore order. Once he had the backing of the people, Athaliah was dethroned and killed. The threat of idolatry overtaking Judah was extinguished and a great fundraising project was established to repair the Temple. The glory of Jehovah was placed back where it belonged. All of this was made possible because of a little boy who was willing to give all the glory to his God.

### Afflicted for Righteousness

It is one thing to be afflicted for failing God; it is another thing to be afflicted for righteousness' sake. You would think that doing the right thing at the right time would help you evade any kind of affliction at all. It is amazing the flak that will come your way when all you have done is obey God's voice. Consider what the apostle Peter wrote to us:

*Yet if anyone suffers as a Christian, let him not be ashamed, but let him glorify God in this matter.*
(1 Peter 4:16)

Although the Scripture above began with the word if, there are no ifs, ands, or buts in the Christian life. It is a foregone conclusion that if you will live godly in Christ, you will suffer persecution (2 Timothy 3:12). It has always bothered me to hear so-called mighty Christians brag about their blessed lifestyle, free of severe afflictions. The fact of the matter is this, God has always used afflictions to mold us and help us to conform to His ways. Evading these difficult times will eventually come back to haunt us, because all in all our growth in Him will have been stunted. Truth be told, we are constantly offended and ashamed of the sufferings that befall us. The end result is we hold back and don't glorify God in the times of affliction. This disheartening outlook causes those same afflictions to become more mental than anything else, opening the door to deep depression.

At this point, a decision must be made. Are the stresses brought into my life at this present time actually the beginning of the end, or am I being set up for a breakout? It is a similar decision the three Hebrew boys had to make when considering their predicament in Babylonian captivity. Their being in captivity called for wholesale adjustments, ones that would affect every facet of their lives. This included the way they ate, worshiped, and served their God. Their lives took a greater hit when they realized their rights had been taken away completely. To make matters worse, their brethren were not opposed to the new way of life, so their allegiance to Jehovah was sticking out like a sore thumb.

## *Challenged in Captivity*

Their first challenge came in the form of having to eat the king's delicacies, which were unlawful for them. Would Jehovah actually hold them accountable for this eating practice when in captivity? They weren't ready to find out, because in their eyes if it was important to God in the first place, then it would also be important to them. With Daniel's help, they avoided a confrontation with the king by putting together a plan that would allow them to stay faithful to God. The Lord was about to use this lesson in obedience as a springboard to increase their faith. With the ability to humble themselves and limit their diet to something that was found pleasing in God's sight, during this time of affliction, knowledge and skill in all literature and wisdom was given to them. After the test was complete, the king found their wisdom and understanding ten times better than that of his astrologers and magicians. In their eyes, giving glory to God sure had its perks, ones that included a promotion setting them over the affairs of the province of Babylon.

The pressure to conform continued to increase when an order was given to worship Babylon's god. A huge golden image was created for this purpose and the entire kingdom, including the Hebrews, was expected to worship it. The decree forced everyone, at the sound of the instruments, to stop what they were doing to bow down and worship the god made by hands. When their refusal to do so was brought to the king's attention, they were called in for questioning. Daniel was not with them at this time and they could not depend on his wisdom to get them out of this difficulty. They had to stand alone, with their integrity being challenged in public. The king decided to give them another opportunity to rectify their error in judgment. Perhaps he thought that this was a total misunderstanding, because no one would have the audacity to challenge the king's order knowingly. Their response to this second chance was completely unexpected.

> *"O Nebuchadnezzar, we have no need to answer you in this matter. If that is the case, our God whom we serve is able to deliver us from the burning fiery furnace, and He will deliver us from your hand, O king. But if not, let it be known to you, O king, that*

*we do not serve your gods, nor will we worship the gold image which you have set up."*

(Daniel 3:16-18)

Defying a king's order, much less the king himself, was grounds for death by fire. King Nebuchadnezzar had never been challenged by anyone in his kingdom, and he was going to make sure that these Hebrew captives would be made an example of what happened to anyone who defied the king. One last tactic of intimidation did not move them when he threatened to throw them into the fire seven times hotter than it had ever been.

Intimidation has always been an effective weapon used in the hand of our enemy, satan. Coupled with fear and uncertainty, it has its way of oozing into our psyche to make us back down from the promises of God. Fear is most successful when it paralyzes our thinking. Everything becomes cloudy and unclear. Even the simplest of decisions become ever so difficult, causing delays because we just don't want to get it wrong. We have become wishy-washy, hedging on every decision as others lose confidence in our decision-making abilities or as the Scripture says, double-minded and unstable in all our ways (James 1:8). Such is the torment mentioned in Scripture when fear dominates our thoughts (1 John 4:18). The only way to combat fear and intimidation is through confidence in His word.

*So shall I have an answer for him who reproaches me, for I trust in Your word.* (Psalm 119:42)

### A Determining Factor

What was the determining factor that allowed these young men to challenge a king's order with such courageousness? The answer would be found in their faith.

Their faith had just been increased by their first encounter with opposition. But what was even more impressive was their showing of integrity. There was no guarantee that God would save them from the fiery furnace, and yet they were not willing to bow as many of their countrymen had. They had just come out of the furnace of affliction, and victoriously at that. What did it matter to them that this new furnace was to be made seven times hotter? After the Lord had responded to their pleas during the eating incident, they were now ready for the next step. The king was now incensed by their fearlessness, so much so that he revoked the opportunity for a do over. As they were thrown into the fire, Nebuchadnezzar's countenance changed from glee to astonishment.

> *Then King Nebuchadnezzar was astonished; and he rose in haste and spoke, saying to his counselors, "Did we not cast three men bound into the midst of the fire?" They answered and said to the king, "True, O king." "Look!" he answered, "I see four men loose, walking in the midst of the fire; and they are not hurt, and the form of the fourth is like the Son of God."* (Daniel 3:24-25)

The Lord not only delivered them from all harm, but not a hair was singed, their clothes were not affected, not even the smell of fire was noticeable. Little did Nebuchadnezzar know that he had played right into God's hands. In God's kingdom, furnaces of affliction are not to be feared because it is what God uses to produce and find hidden jewels.

Entering into a furnace of affliction is more than a one-time experience. No one is completely refined the first time. The process needs to be repeated over and over and over again. As we continue to live our lives in God, there will be times of negligence and even an occasional slipup that will sever our relationship with Him. It is then needful for us to enter into that furnace of affliction to set things right before Him. We could start out right with a great beginning, but unless we sustain it in the presence of the Lord, we can lose what God's grace brought to our lives when we were undeserving.

### Joash's Costly Mistake

Negligence in the things of the Lord is what caused Joash's ending to be quite different from his beginning. When the people of God decided to hide him away, shielding him from the influences of his carnal father's regime, never in their wildest imagination did they believe Joash would end his life in this manner. When Jehoiada died, so did the king's faithfulness to Jehovah. Without the leading and guiding of his mentor, he found easier ways of living his life and a more comfortable lifestyle, if you will. His love for the Temple and being in the presence of God began to wane. His visits to the house of God became less frequent and he lost his spiritual edge. His heart was drawn away to other gods; ones who helped him push aside the one and only true God, Jehovah. That was the beginning of his downfall. He would never be able to recover from this devastating loss. His death came by assassination, hidden away in his bedroom where no one else could see. Isn't it ironic that as a baby he was hidden initially, to do great works in the kingdom of God? His death only confirmed that in the end, his life was directed *away* from God and not *to* Him. At life's end, this precious jewel of a man lost all of his luster and shine. His life ended in tragedy because he wouldn't let the furnace of affliction completely purify his life in the Lord.

The only thing separating a Christian today from becoming a vessel of honor is the furnace of affliction. Although it has been predetermined that our lives in Him will be successful, we all must go through that furnace of affliction to be refined and purified. It is the process God has chosen to dig us out of the rough and refine us in ways that will leave a clear and unmistakable impression of Him in our life. Won't you let the furnace of affliction bring you out of hiding to let the rest of the world see what God has known and seen all along? You truly are a jewel that will bring honor to His name. Just burn, baby, burn!

# CHAPTER 3
## Battle Scars

*Woe is me for my hurt! My wound is severe. But I say, "Truly this is an infirmity, and I must bear it."*
(Jeremiah 10:19)

Scars, generally speaking, will leave a mark or indentation resulting from an injury. Much like afflictions, they can be either physical (i.e. , body scars), emotional, or moral. As we accumulate more and more scars in the rigors of life, there are some we are proud of, whereas there are others we would totally like to forget.

Playing football in high school was such a testosterone-driven experience. There were so many little obsessions that we couldn't avoid that ultimately drove us incessantly to pursue them. These obsessions would eventually prove our manhood. One such obsession was getting as many stick marks on your helmet as humanly possible. A stick mark was received whenever you collided with another player, head to head. The harder the collision, the more paint rubbed off the other players' helmet onto yours. If your helmet had a myriad of colors other than your own, it was the physical personification of a great hitter. That being said, because I was a placekicker with very little time spent on the field, plus the fact that I could not legally be hit in most cases, my helmet was completely clean. In my junior year, something happened on an extra point that would change all of that. My holder bobbled the ball, which I picked up, forcing me to run for the goal line. As I prepared myself to get hit for the first time ever, it wasn't as bad as I had imagined. When I came back to the sideline, everybody was whooping it up because there was a stick mark of gold on my helmet. For the next week or so, the razzing continued nonstop. Although my stick mark had been placed by another player's hit on me, nevertheless, it was something to be proud of.

### *Forgettable Scars*

There are other scars received on the battlefield that are a greater mark emotionally than those found on the body. My heart went out to an elderly gentleman when he approached me after the service one day. He was a Vietnam War veteran and had served his country proudly. If he had to do it all over again, nothing would have changed. He would've gladly made the same sacrifices so that we as a country would remain free. The thing about our conversation that saddened me the most was his prayer request. He had admitted to me that for more than fifty years, the nightmares of atrocities experienced in Vietnam continued to haunt him. No matter what he tried, they still found a way to bother his sleep. He was hoping that by some miracle God could relieve him from this torture to help him finally rest in peace. As he walked away,

## Battle Scars

limping into the night, I realized there were greater emotional issues he was fighting than the physical ones I could see with my own eyes.

Our battles with the enemy, satan, will be never-ending. We must realize that quitting is not on his agenda. His time to deceive as many as he can is coming to a swift end and his treachery increases by the minute. Because of his tenacity, when in battle we need to accept that somewhere, sometime, somehow we will be wounded. It has nothing to do with faulty weaponry or poorly planned strategies. It will happen to the best of us. It is the part of war that is completely unavoidable. When the wounds become so severe that they cause hardship or discomfort, keep in mind they are only afflictions, which by definition puts them in a temporary category. God has everything under control from the outset, and it will only be a matter of time before His will breaks through.

*Many are the afflictions of the righteous but the LORD delivers him out of them all.* (Psalms 34:19)

The passage of Scripture in Jeremiah at the beginning of the chapter begins somewhat morbidly. His first words were, woe is me, and my wound is severe. In other words, he tried to convey the impression that the wound was so deep that it would leave a scar that would make a full recovery impossible. I'm sure that when satan surveyed Jeremiah's situation, he also came to the same conclusion that this battle was now over. Chalk one up to the god of this world. The most intriguing portion of the Scripture comes immediately after uttering such words of defeat. Between breaths, he, Jeremiah, does an about-face that changes his outlook 180°. His words of despair turned into words of determination. How in the world could his thoughts change so dramatically in such a short period of time? It is a job that only the word of God could do.

### The Power of the Word

*For the word of God is quick, and powerful, and sharper than any two-edged sword, piercing even to the dividing asunder of soul and spirit, and of the joints and marrow, and is a discerner of the thoughts and intents of the heart.* (Hebrews 4:12KJV)

There is nothing quicker nor more powerful than the word of God. It is so sharp it can find its way into the most intimate parts of our being (i.e., soul and spirit) and divide it as an expert butcher would divide his most expensive meats. As formidable as that sounds its power to discern our thoughts and the intents of our heart is even more extraordinary.

From Jeremiah's actions, we can speculate that God gave him a word he put into action, giving him new life similar to what the word did for David.

*This is my comfort in my affliction, for Your word has given me life.... I remembered your judgments of old, O LORD, and have comforted myself.*
(Psalms 119:50, 52)

The difficulties Jeremiah had to face are no different than what must be dealt with in our battles against the enemy. From the beginning of time, God's people have, at one time or another had to confront adversity completely alone, depending solely on God and His word. It is in confronting these difficulties that most of us have had to pull ourselves up by our bootstraps and encourage ourselves. Ostracized from the rest of the church, we were left alone with our thoughts, having to depend on His word. Now with his thoughts in check, Jeremiah could look at his afflictions in a completely different light. He could then agree with David when he made this boast:

*Unless your law had been my delight, I would then have perished in my affliction.* (Psalms 119:92)

Delighting in God's law is proof positive that perishing during a time of affliction can be avoided. His word will prove to become a lamp unto our feet and a light unto our pathway (Psalms 119:105).

### Ruth's Powerful Testimony

Ruth was a woman from the Old Testament who could surely identify with Jeremiah and his afflictions. In a short period of time, she had lost her husband, her father-in-law, and her brother-in-law. Her mother-in-law, Naomi, had moved with her husband and sons to Ruth's country, Moab, only because of a great famine that had destroyed her nation's crops. With all of the men dead in her family and the economic situation becoming more stable back home, Naomi felt it was the right time to go back to her homeland. The deaths of her husband and sons had left such an emotional impact that the scars that were left cut really deep. Without uttering a word, she allowed bitterness to set in, so much so that it began to destroy her from the inside out.

As Naomi was making her way back to Bethlehem, she was able to convince one daughter-in-law, Orpah, to stay in Moab. She had no such luck with the other daughter-in-law, Ruth. The decision to leave with Naomi had great consequences. Leaving with her mother-in-law would have demonstrated a great amount of faith. First of all,

Bethlehem was not her origin of birth and the Hebrew nation was not her people. Most important, Jehovah was not the God who she served. Leaving Moab would also validate her deep love for Naomi.

> *But Ruth said: "Entreat me not to leave you, or to turn back from following after you; for wherever you go, I will go; and wherever you lodge, I will lodge; your people shall be my people, and your God, my God. Where you die, I will die, and there will I be buried. The LORD do so to me, and more also, if anything but death parts you and me."*
>
> (Ruth 1:16-17)

I'm pretty sure Ruth's scars were as deep and severe as those of Naomi, yet her husband's death was not enough to sever their relationship. Ruth was willing to start a new life in a faraway land because of an indelible mark, a scar if you will, that her husband left on her. She had been treated royally as a queen, and Ruth understood that her husband's treatment of her was the result of his relationship with his God. For all of the people who she knew throughout her lifetime, Naomi was the only one who could connect her to her husband's God. Her decision to go with Naomi would cement that possibility, and she would not miss it for the world. For all of her heartbreak and her cluelessness in explaining these painful losses, everything was beginning to make sense. Only through her afflictions and her severe wounds would an opportunity of a lifetime present itself. Again, like David, she had found purpose in her afflictions.

> *It is good for me that I have been afflicted, that I may learn your statutes. The law of your mouth is*

*better to me than thousands of coins of gold and silver.* (Psalms 119:71-72)

In assessing her life to this point, she decided to make a conscious decision that would follow her as long as she lived. Life had dealt her a bad hand, but regardless, she would bear it. Would her decision make the rest of her life less painful? No, not really, it would only make life more bearable.

Ruth's decision was now ready to be put to the test. With no familiarity to boost her confidence, her "spiritual boot camp" was about to begin. In God's Army, our training always includes some type of affliction. Cognizant of that fact, we should never be surprised by it.

*Beloved, do not think it strange concerning the fiery trial which is to try you, as though some strange thing happened to you; but rejoice to the extent that you partake of Christ's sufferings, that when His glory is revealed, you may also be glad with exceeding joy.* (1 Peter 4:12-13)

Naomi's handling of afflictions never did her any favors. She never got to the point of fully embracing them, and subsequently lost out on the greater blessings God had planned for her life. The one characteristic that blocked the Lord from allowing His mercy to have its full impact was her bitterness. Unbeknownst to many, her bitterness ran deeper than her scars. Bitterness had enough of a stranglehold on her that changing her name from Naomi to Mara was no big deal. Living in a time when naming a child meant something, Naomi was very glib about the whole name change. It did not move her one iota that she would now be addressed as "bitterness," and no longer "sweetness," as she had been called originally from birth.

I remember a friend of mine, who I had known for many years, doing the same thing. He had a beautiful biblical name attached to his life, one that if he chose to live up to it would bring great honor unto God. After the initial shock wore off, the new name chosen really wasn't all that bad. The thing that hurt me the most was the timing of the name change. For all of the years that I had known him, one of his better qualities was his tenacity in never giving up in the things of God. For whatever reasons, the change in his name came after one of the most devastating times in his spiritual life. Sad to say, bitterness became his best friend, one that would be able to control him in ways that were nonexistent in the past. With bitterness now in control, cynicism and a critical spirit would get on board to enjoy the ride to disaster.

### Ruth Takes a Stand

Ruth would have none of it. "Woe is me" would never become a part of her vocabulary. She would never let herself stoop that low, because the word of God had started to affect her like nothing had in her entire life. Learning God's statutes produced the courage to live up to her name in a time of unyielding affliction. Ruth means: friend, friendship. Her true purpose in life was to be friendly and make friends even in the darkest and dreariest times of her life. It was the grace of God, ultimately, that helped her to respond to her severe wounds in a godly fashion. When others she encountered found out the great losses she had to overcome and how she was able to handle it with such grace, it drew people to her, making it that much easier to befriend them.

## Battle Scars

*A man who has friends must himself be friendly...*
*(Proverbs 18:24)*

Ruth's disposition and outlook in life had allowed her to become a great asset to her mother-in-law, Naomi. Her work ethic not only brought financial stability to the household, her temperament was such a positive influence on Naomi that it had an impact on her character as well. It was then that Naomi came out of her funk and began to instruct Ruth on how to find a husband. It was only a short time later that Ruth met her future husband, Boaz. It was a match made in heaven of sorts, much like the fairytales, and she lived happily ever after. Were her battle scars eventually removed? Not likely, but neither were they a hindrance for God to bless her in the way He did.

As we have seen, dealing with battle scars is a delicate proposition. It can be compared to walking through a minefield, one that with any misstep can produce losses that can be irrecoverable. More times than not, physically speaking, doctors can nurse one back to health if given the chance. Modern medicine has made such great strides in that area that we can leave the hospital knowing eventually everything will get back to normal. Recovering emotionally is another story. One of the greatest lies we have accepted from our childhood is the little jingle we used to sing: sticks and stones may break my bones but names will never hurt me. If only that were true, and were that simple, it would settle a lot of hurts. But the fact of the matter is we know it is not true, and emotional scars caused by words from our childhood still haunt us today.

A major problem in dealing with afflictions is when they are both physical and emotional in nature. The affliction then becomes a double-edged sword, wielding its power with sharper more powerful thrusts. It is an error on our part to believe that one affliction always replaces the other, because we can encounter situations where they work hand-in-hand to make the affliction more severe. From personal experience, I know this to be a fact.

### My Thorn in the Flesh

At the writing of this chapter, I am at the height of my evangelistic ministry. It has been a slow and deliberate move of God to get me to where I am today. Because it is a ministry of miracles being dispersed upon people in an everyday fashion, I have received a thorn in the flesh to keep my life in check. A messenger of satan has been allowed to buffet me, similar to the one the apostle Paul had dealt with.

> *And lest I should be exalted above measure by the abundance of the revelations, a thorn in the flesh was given to me, a messenger of Satan to buffet me, lest I be exalted above measure.*
> 
> (2 Corinthians 12:7)

This thorn has begun in the physical, which makes a lot of sense, because after suffering the effects of polio pretty much all my life, satan could continue the damage in my body as his starting point. Originally, the polio had affected my body only from the waist up. My lower extremities were never affected, and it allowed me to play sports up to the point of winning a football scholarship on the university level. It is only now that my lower body is starting to suffer the same effects that the rest of my body has always had to deal with. Slowly but surely, different parts of my body are starting to shut down, and doctors do not have a clue as to what is going on. It has altered my sleeping habits, the way I eat and what I eat, and even the way I walk has been

## Battle Scars

included. Nothing I do physically comes easily anymore, from the time that I get up till the time I go to bed. Let me give you some examples. In the morning: washing up (putting soap and shaving cream on my face, I cannot turn on certain showers), getting dressed (there are times I cannot button my shirts, put on my socks, or tie my shoes), using my hands and feet (there are times I cannot open a door, unscrew a bottle cap, open the hood on my car, going up and down stairs is becoming more of a challenge, my jogging is slower than most people can walk).

The difficulty in completing tasks that most people don't think twice about has made its way into my mind and emotionally in my heart. As my physical struggles have become daily chores, my mind has to work harder to make up for my physical deficiencies. At the end of the day, I find myself emotionally spent and somewhat frustrated, because as hard as I have worked, it appears that I have not accomplished much. You would think that the underlying benefit of such tiredness would allow me to knock out the entire night in a restful sleep. I wish! I rarely sleep more than four hours at a time, and many times it is spent on a recliner away from my wife.

What boggles my mind more than anything else is the fact that the Lord is moving more powerfully in our ministry than ever before. The miracles are not only increasing in number but in intensity as well. It is common to see the Lord heal people of things like cancer, tumors, fibromyalgia, spinal stenosis and the like. God has unstopped deaf ears, opened blinded eyes, and has grown out legs that were inches shorter than the other. There have been times I have dealt with folks suffering from diseases I have never heard of and could not pronounce for the life of me. All in all, God deals with them and heals them according to His will and their faith. Once I have completed my assignment for the day, things go back to the way they were and I find myself a complete mess.

### My Greatest Fear

What I write next can be confirmed by my wife, because she has had to deal firsthand with my negative responses to my physical and emotional afflictions. Initially, I did not handle it well. Oh, how I identified with Jeremiah when he talked about his woe and how his wounds were so severe. Because my pains became more chronic in nature, I found myself to be continually cranky and impatient. My wife was taking the brunt of my ire, and it began to scare me half to death. I was afraid that one day she would get so fed up that she would leave and never come back. I could not believe that I had fallen so far. I did not like looking in the mirror, because I did not like what I saw. But how was I going to get back to the place in God that I had been in for so many years? I felt that the wounds were digging deeper with each and every day, and the scars were being more deep-rooted in my heart. It was then that I began to cry out to God, just like David.

> *I am afflicted very much; Revive me, O LORD, according to Your word.* (Psalms 119:107)

It did not take the Lord very long to respond to my petition, but never did I think that His response would be as such.

> *Surely He has borne our griefs and carried our sorrows; Yet we esteemed Him stricken, Smitten by God, and afflicted. But He was wounded for our transgressions, He was bruised for our iniquities;*

## Battle Scars

*The chastisement for our peace was upon Him, and by His stripes we are healed.* (Isaiah 53:4-5)

He wanted me to be assured that my sorrows had already been taking care of. The stripes He bore on His back allowed Him to confirm His membership into the fraternity of the afflicted. But the object lesson He was trying to teach by bringing these Scriptures to my attention was the simple fact that whether I was crippled or completely whole physically, His wounds and bruises, coupled with His death, allowed me the opportunity for salvation that I could never attain on my own. Although the afflictions placed upon Him were unmerited and completely unjustified, He was willing to give His life anyway so that a dying world could be saved. The odd thing about being delivered from His afflictions was that it did not come until after His death. It was the only way that His plan would work.

After being humbled by His response, a final decision had to be made and this is what I finally decided. Whether He heals me or not, no matter how severe the afflictions would continue, my new mantra would be, "I will bear it." My battle scars now have new meaning and I can go on living my life in peace.

*but rejoice to the extent that you partake of Christ's sufferings, that when His glory is revealed, you may also be glad with exceeding joy.* (1 Peter 4:13)

I would like to close this chapter with a quote from one of my favorite preachers, T. F. Tenney. I once heard him say this in a sermon, "Never trust a man who walks without a limp." These are wise words coming from a very wise man. My final question to you then is this, are your battle scars a source of pride, or do you hide them from embarrassment? Rejoice in the fact that God has allowed you and me to be partakers of His sufferings. There is an eternal benefit that is just too good to pass up.

*If we suffer, we shall also reign with him:*
*(2 Timothy 2:12 KJV)*

# CHAPTER 4

## The Unknown Soldier

*You therefore must endure hardship as a good soldier of Jesus Christ* (2 Timothy 2:3)

From the time I was a little boy, every once in a while I would hear of an "Unknown Soldier" who was being honored by our country. It was usually at the time of Memorial Day or Labor Day that the subject popped up, and I kind of knew what was being talked about, but only vaguely. It wasn't until I actually took some time to study the history of the "Unknown Soldier" that I fully understood the impact this tradition had on our country.

The honor originated in 1921 after World War I. One soldier was selected amongst four from different battlegrounds in different parts of the world. After being exhumed, they were transported from Europe to the United States. After one of these brave soldiers had been chosen to represent all of the unknown soldiers who had given their lives for their country, a tomb was created for him. In subsequent wars, an "Unknown Soldier" was chosen as well. There are now four unknown soldiers buried in Arlington National Cemetery, one for each world war, the Korean conflict, and the Vietnam War. In actuality, because of technology the last soldier's identity is known.[5]

The attention and honor given to them is remarkable. A Sentinel guards the tomb twenty-four hours a day, seven days a week. Totally prepared for intrusion, the Sentinel bears his weapon away from the tomb. While on duty, the Sentinel crosses a sixty-three-foot rubber surfaced walkway in exactly twenty-one steps. He then faces the tomb for twenty-one seconds, and turns again, and pauses an additional twenty-one seconds before retracing his steps. The number twenty-one is symbolic of the highest salute accorded to dignitaries in military and state ceremonies. For me, the inscription on the tomb is its most impressive feature. The inscription reads, "Here Rests in Honored Glory, An American Soldier Known but to God." For all of the decorated war heroes in our history, to this day the "Unknown Soldier" receives our highest honor and respect.[6]

As we turn our focus now to judgment day, God's honored glory will be bestowed upon only those known to Him. I am sure we have a picture in our mind as to who those people will be, yet we will be totally surprised when the greatest rewards will be handed out by our Master. Somewhat similar to the honor given to the "Unknown Soldier," there will be folks we had never ever heard of who will make their way to the front of the line to receive God's best. They never had a platform ministry, much less any oratory skills. Working in the shadows behind the scenes was good enough for them, and they really didn't care at the end of the day who received credit for the work that had been done. They worked tirelessly, going completely unnoticed or even worse, unappreciated. Because their job never involved the spotlight, the importance of their labor was lost in the brilliance of platform ministry. Mention their name, and it doesn't ring a bell, but God certainly knows who they are and what they have done. The reason why God is so enamored with them is because the limelight was never pursued by them. The privilege of working for Him in His kingdom was enough inspiration to do what no one else was willing to do, (i.e., the dirty work). Dealing with afflictions and seasons of difficulty would not hinder them and they could always be counted on to not only complete a work, but to do it with all diligence. If you're really keeping count of the amount of afflictions and their severity they would have to endure, not to mention the determination to see them through, you would have to agree that they were light years ahead of everyone else. Yet, only the Lord could truly say that He knew who they were.

### One of the First Unknown Soldiers

It is one of these spiritual "Unknown Soldiers" who I would like to write about today. At first glance, her name is somewhat uncommon and even more so difficult to spell. I think attempting to pronounce it causes an even greater challenge, and I'm sure throughout her entire life very few people could say her name correctly. As I dug deeper into the meaning of her name, upon further examination I found out that the combination used to form her name was quite fascinating. Literally her name means, "Jehovah her Glory."[7] My studies showed that she was the first person in Scripture to have a name compounded with the name of God (Jehovah). What was even more astounding was the fact that this name was given to a woman. Living in Old Testament times meant that women would be treated just a little better than slaves. What makes her name even more mind-boggling was the fact that the Jewish nation had such a fear and reverence for the name of their God that they would not even pronounce it in public, for fear of pronouncing it wrong. The name Yahweh was substituted for Jehovah to keep everyone in check. The question we must then ask ourselves is this, was her anonymity a mere coincidence or was it divinely intended? Who was this woman of God with such a strange name? She was none other than the mother of Moses, Jochebed.

She lived her life at a time when Israel was in captivity. If being enslaved by the Egyptians was not bad enough, the decree given by their Pharaoh brought even more affliction to her. By pronouncement of the Pharaoh, all male Hebrew babies were to be put to death, and her newborn boy fell under that category. She understood fully that if she had decided to hide him from impending death and was to be found out, not only would the baby lose his life but she would have to forfeit her life as well. It was a predicament that no one, much less a mother, would ever want to deal with. If there was ever a no-win situation, it was here.

Making that decision would have been so much easier if she would've had any kind of divine intervention. Unlike Mary, the mother of Jesus, there was no angel delivering messages to assure her that this unlikely pregnancy was divinely inspired. She could not depend on prophecies given in Scripture that foretold the greatness of her little boy. The confirmations in the heavens with stars and angelic hosts were never made available to her to lift up her faith. Nevertheless, a decision had to be made. She needed clarity of mind to be able to survey any other options, if available.

This much she understood. She was in a foreign land, without any kind of rights. She was up against a ruthless,

## *The Unknown Soldier*

jealous Pharaoh with a loyal following, determined to destroy the Hebrew nation. If Pharaoh's decree were to be defiantly disobeyed, that defiance in and of itself would be considered a death wish. What would make this situation even more nerve-wracking would be the fact that she would have to put her motherly instincts on hold and do something that would appear heartless. She had a cockamamie idea that she could save her son if she were to build a mini ark, placing him inside it on the Nile River, and wait for something good to happen. Any outsider looking in would have come to the conclusion that this woman had completely lost it. Who in their right mind would honestly believe that an ark would be the means God would use to create a miracle? If the crocodiles did not eat him first, surely the currents of the river would overturn the ark and the baby would drown.

### *Being Put in the Hands of God*

Why was she so willing to put her baby's life in the hands of fate? But this "Unknown Soldier" had a better understanding of the situation than we do after the fact. She was not putting her baby in the hands of fate; she in reality was putting her baby in the hands of God. Her courage demonstrated in the time of affliction undoubtedly helped her live up to her name, "Jehovah her Glory." It was shortly after the ark found itself floating down the Nile River that the miracle began to unfold. As Pharaoh's daughter was bathing herself, the little ark nudged its way close enough to be seen by her in the distance. Her curiosity got the better of her and she commanded her servants to bring the ark for a closer look. As she opened the ark, never had she gazed upon such a beautiful baby. Although she knew it was a Hebrew baby, the baby found grace in her sight and she decided to keep him. This is where divine providence began to show itself. She actually hired Jochebed to nurse him.

Her new job, although placed back in the shadows, would provide an opportunity not only to nurse her child, but to raise him in the ways of the Lord. She understood that because the Lord was merciful enough to save Moses from impending death, there had to be a special call on his life. With that in mind, she made sure that the oracles of God would be taught in such a way that the foundation she was providing would never allow him to forget his God. This behind the scenes assignment now paralleled the assignment given to Mary, the mother of Jesus. And like Mary, she would do anything in her power to raise her boy right. Unlike Mary, future generations would not give her the same honor. In actuality, she would be forgotten rather quickly. At the end of her life and the culmination of her assignment, she truly fit the definition of an "Unknown Soldier." I don't really know if there's any kind of inscription where she is buried, but if so, it should read, "Here Rests in Honored Glory a Child of the King Known but to God."

All through the history of mankind, the Lord has reserved a place in heaven for many "Unknown Soldiers." Even through the dark ages when religion was mostly non-existent, the Lord has always had a remnant of believers willing to lift up His holy name. The fact that they are unknown to us means little to Him, because they are the ones He has used in the background and in the shadows to keep the truth from being extinct. My generation (born in the 50s) has had its share of heroes, those who have inspired us to serve God more faithfully. It has been their example we have used to sustain our lives in God when the most severe of afflictions were trying to destroy us. One such person who has had such an impact on my life in so

## The Unknown Soldier

many different ways was my grandmother on my mother's side.

### A Modern Day Unknown Soldier

Frances Hernandez is not a name that will ring anyone's bell. If there was ever a woman who lived her life in anonymity, it was she. At first glance, she appeared to be the typical Hispanic woman, somewhat shy but very hard-working. If there was a Scripture that modeled her life, it would be this one:

*Whatever your hand finds to do, do it with your might; for there is no work or device or knowledge or wisdom in the grave where you are going.*
(Ecclesiastes 9:10)

I don't know if she had a premonition that her life in this world was to be cut short when she took advantage of every waking hour, using her hands to be a blessing to whomever she crossed paths with.

The meaning of her name gives us some insight as to what kind of person she was. Frances means: generous, giving. I know that almost any grandmother living today would fall under that particular category. But at the same rate, there was something about her and her life that helped me to see that her giving was above and beyond the call of duty. I know personally she had a great impact on my life and did something that I don't think she did for the other grandchildren she loved so much. We would play a little game when Grandpa was away at work. She would allow me into their bedroom to look under the bed on the side that my grandfather slept on. I was given so much time to look under the bed where his extra change would fall from his pants to the floor while he was reading his Bible. I could take with me whatever I could hold in my little hands. I found out later from one of my aunties that she would pretty much do the same thing when he was not around. She would take the change she would find, store it in a safe place, and when she had enough it would be taken to church to give to the missionaries.

Amongst the many challenges she would face, playing the role of "family peacemaker" was perhaps her most taxing. Attending to nine children and becoming the buffer between them and their gruff daddy was no easy task. The wisdom to say the right thing at the right time surely was God-inspired. The calming effect she had on those she had the opportunity to minister to was incredible. Financially making ends meet was a feat to behold. She had ways of stretching a dollar like you had never seen, and there were times the family's money really had to stretch. But it was her desire to see her children saved that turned out to be the greatest challenge of her life.

### Her Greatest Challenges in Life

The afflictions in her life were many, but there are two that stood out head and shoulders over anything else she had to deal with. My perception of my grandmother, who died when I was nine years old, was of a lady who was always sick. Again, when I spoke to one of my aunties, she confirmed that to be a fact. She was thin in stature and somewhat frail. She suffered with various ailments, but it was the arthritis that caused her most of the pain. When she contracted leukemia, cancer of the blood, it was the one disease that she would not be able to overcome.

It was during this time period her oldest son brought her the greatest of heartaches. He had been raised in the ways of the Lord, but when he got old enough to leave the home he did so without any intentions of serving God. To

## The Unknown Soldier

make that decision less obvious, he joined the military for a stint in the Army, and when that was completed he came back to the United States to live a life on the streets in gang activity. He rose through the ranks in a local gang to become the ringleader, and he was somewhat ruthless. He was good at leading others because this lifestyle had become his passion, and alcohol mixed with drugs became his god. My recollection of him as I was growing up was of a man who caused a great ruckus when every once in a while he would come to my grandma's house to visit. His visits would always leave my grandmother nervous and upset. Only a mother could truly understand what I'm about to write about parents dealing with wayward children. There's something about a mother's never giving up attitude that allows her to continue touching the throne of God in prayer, knowing that by the grace of God her petition will not only be heard, but answered as well.

Her greatest weapon, which goes without saying, was her prayer life. The daily connection she made with her God was her life. Many would have looked at her, the fact that she was cooped up in her house because of her physical ailments, and would have felt sorry for her. She took advantage of her time alone to spend quality time in the presence of the Master. She was my first example of what a true prayer warrior is all about. After my mom and dad divorced, Grandma was the one that took care of us while Mom went out to work for the first time. In arriving at her house after school, I was usually the first one home. As I wandered around the entire house looking for her, if when I walked into the house the stereo was blazing with gospel music, I knew exactly where she was. She would escape into a room right behind the living room where the stereo was placed. She would play her music somewhat loud, but it would not stop her from lifting her voice, giving that stereo competition while she was worshiping God in other tongues. I would put my ear up to the door and when I heard her loudly praising God in her prayer language, I felt a sense of peace and I knew that everything was all right.

As my uncle's gang involvement became more intense, her fear for his life grew by leaps and bounds. I remember my mom telling me God would wake Grandma up in the wee hours of the morning to intercede for her boy. She later found out it was at that particular time he was involved in hostile shootouts. As she prayed to the Lord to put a hedge of protection on him, he was never wounded, much less killed like some of his fellow gang members. There were countless times she was woken up at all hours of the night where she continued with the same assignment, praying for David because he was in trouble. There were times her heart wanted to burst in agony, but she just could not quit, it was too important and somebody had to take on the responsibility to pray for him. Nobody knew she was going to this extreme to pray for his salvation, but God knew, and God knew her. Although it would take some time for the answer to come, I believe that when she put her music on and escaped quietly into that room, the Lord was already there, ready to listen to her cries. She was a good soldier, because good soldiers always endure hardships.

### This Prayer Made All the Difference in the World

She was not the only one after her son, because the battle for his soul would intensify and the enemy was willing to pull out all the stops to make sure she would stop praying for him. That would mean her physical afflictions would become more pronounced. The medications prescribed to lessen the arthritic pain were losing their strength. She was also losing the battle with the leukemia.

## *The Unknown Soldier*

Her body was well-worn and beaten down, her mind emotionally spent. When the Lord decided not to alleviate the pain of the arthritis and free her from the weakening of her body because of the leukemia, she made a decision in prayer that would change the course of not only her life, but that of her son as well. Her one and only prayer became this, "Please don't let me die until I see my son saved." No matter how long it would take, no matter what she had to endure, it would be the prayer she would offer until she got an answer, or died trying.

What I am about to write happened over fifty years ago, and yet in my mind it is as clear as if it would've happened yesterday. A group of the grandchildren were playing in the front yard next door to Grandma's. As we were running around as we normally did, my Uncle David's car drove up and parked just outside the driveway of my grandmother's house. I'm not sure how long he waited, but the entire family was in the car, hoping that grandma's arrival would not be too long. As she and my grandfather rolled into the driveway, my uncle hurriedly got out of the car, running up to her as she approached the porch.

He said, "Mom, you won't believe this, but God filled me with the Holy Ghost at home."

Her shocked look said it all. "David," she uttered angrily, "don't be fooling around like that, that isn't funny."

He began to recount the experience to her as she gazed upon him in disbelief. While under the influence of heroin and alcohol, he had begun to feel his life slipping away. He called out to God in these exact words, "God! I'm dying! Have mercy on me." When she finally realized he was telling her the truth, she burst out in tears, hugged him tightly, and as he returned her hug, they both simultaneously began to speak in other tongues, right there on the porch. He was later baptized in the name of Jesus in

October 1963. It was just over a year later that she finally succumbed to leukemia, dying at the tender age of fifty-three. It has been years since I have gone back to the gravesite, and to tell you the truth, I really don't remember what had been written on her gravestone. But knowing now what I know about my grandmother and what a great soldier in God's Army she was, I believe it would have been appropriate to write as an epitaph, "Here Rests in Honored Glory a Child of the King Known but to God."

### The Fruit of Her Labor

In truth, she was not delivered from her afflictions until her death. With her new immortal body in heaven, there is no pain or suffering. The agonies of her past life are just that, past. But what became of the son she pretty much gave her life for, enduring these hardships as a good soldier? Rev. David Hernandez became one of the most influential men in the Christian world after receiving the Holy Ghost. Pastoring one of the largest Hispanic churches in the Los Angeles area, he set out to make a difference in the lives of those who had suffered great afflictions. He was both an innovator and a visionary. His childlike faith took him to places that more studied and experienced men feared to go. Understanding that breaking away from a gang lifestyle was nearly impossible, he courageously opened the first drug and alcohol rehabilitation center in his church organization. Criticism and ridicule would not stop him from obeying the voice of God. He later opened a Christian school, followed by a Christian daycare center. In my eyes, the greatest impact he had on his organization was the passion he demonstrated for praise and worship. In essence, he became the father of the "praise and worship" group, with his influence so far-reaching that it changed the culture of an entire organization. In later

## The Unknown Soldier

years, his sanctuary choir would become an extension of himself, winning various awards in choir competitions.

As much as an impact his life in God became, it was all made possible through the sacrifices of an "Unknown Soldier." I would not be surprised if, on judgment day, the reward she receives is greater than his or any of us who minister in the limelight. God has ways of rewarding the efforts of His children who have been lost in the shadows. They may be unknown to us, but in God's eyes they are not only valiant and courageous, but highly appreciated as well.

# CHAPTER 5

## In the Eye of the Beholder

*...God, who gives life to the dead and calls those things which do not exist as though they did;*
(Romans 4:17)

Everything in this world is relative. No matter how much you kick and scream about the things you believe in this world, nothing is absolute. By absolute I mean nothing and no one is perfect, except of course the Lord Jesus Christ. Depending on who is looking at it will pretty much determine whether it is good, bad, pretty, or ugly. Back in the 60s when I was a kid, there was a sitcom that I remember called "The Munsters." It was a program that depicted the family life of these particular ghoulish-looking people. Amongst them you could find characters that looked like Frankenstein's monster, vampires, or werewolves. They lived in a haunted house that was as creepy inside as it was out. The reason I make mention of this particular program is because of one family member who was considered "the ugly duckling." She was the only one of the family (actually a niece of the mother) who did not have ghoulish physical features. She was somewhat of a Marilyn Monroe look-alike (her character's name was Marilyn Munster), yet in their eyes she was distressingly unattractive. The family viewed Marilyn's appearance as an affliction, but still treated her with kindness and love. Marilyn herself was all too aware of her "homeliness," and bemoaned the fact that she kept scaring off potential boyfriends, having no clue that the young men were in fact frightened away by her monstrous family.[8] Now then, who was right, the family or the prospective boyfriends? Truly, beauty was in the eye of the beholder.

### The Only Opinion That Matters

In evaluating who we are and what we are living for God, the only viewpoint we should ever take into consideration as absolute is that of the Lord Jesus Christ. In actuality, His opinion is the only one that really matters because He doesn't waver, neither does He hesitate. He's not affected by styles, customs, traditions, or fads. He sees things one way, and there is a good reason for doing so. He wants to make sure that we are given a future with hope.

> *For I know the thoughts that I think toward you, says the LORD, thoughts of peace and not of evil, to give you a future and a hope. Then you will call upon Me and go and pray to Me, and I will listen to you. And you will seek Me and find Me, when you search for Me with all your heart.*
> (Jeremiah 29:11-14)

For that simple reason, He takes His time in meditation, thinking about us. What's even more encouraging is that according to Jeremiah, His thoughts about us our peaceful ones, ones that do not include any kind of evil whatsoever. This hope and future can be literally translated as a cord used for binding.[9] In laymen's terms, the answer we will receive from heaven will be personally signed, sealed, and delivered. What more could one ask for in a God who is trying to convince us that all of heaven is on our side and willing to open its floodgates to pour out a blessing we will not be able to contain? What is even more impressive about our God is the fact that in our times of weakness and disobedience, He can still be found faithful.

*If we are faithless, He remains faithful; He cannot deny Himself.* (2 Timothy 2:13)

That could only mean our Lord and Savior is in it for the long haul and is totally confident that He could bring us to a level of victorious living that He has promised from the very beginning.

Now then, our part in this whole covenant must be put to work. When we come to the understanding of where God is in our lives, we must humble ourselves in prayer and seek Him with a whole heart. The key word in this passage is seek. In seeking God, it becomes more than a casual look. One definition of the word seek is to try to discover.[10] The discovery process in a court case is one where no stone is left unturned. Whichever team of lawyers does the best job at this point will have an added advantage when the case begins. The tenacity of a discoverer is not found in a casual looker. Their ambition to find something or someone is what sets a discoverer apart. A discoverer's ultimate goal is to be that first person to find what no one else has, and he will not stop doing so until successful. That is the kind of doggedness and resolve needed in our search for God. It is then that we will begin to see ourselves the way He sees us, which in turn will make our time spent in His presence not only delightful, but purposeful as well.

### One Form of Sight

Seeing with the naked eye is only one form of sight, and not even the best one at that. On occasion, our eyes have the ability to play tricks on us. We see things that are not really there and our eyesight becomes deceitful. There is a saying that bears repeating, spoken by Benjamin Franklin. *Believe none of what you hear and only half of what you see.*[11] The greatest example of this saying put into practice comes to mind in a speech I heard in high school by NFL referee Jim Tunney. He tried to explain just how difficult it was to referee on the professional level to our football team at our end of the season awards banquet. He placed both hands in front of his chest, with one of them five inches from his chest and the other one five inches in front of the first one. He began to move both hands up and down simultaneously and then asked the question, "Are either of my hands touching each other?" He continued to move his hands in different directions and then asked the question, "Do my hands ever touch my chest?" From our viewpoint, our depth perception was not the best. It appeared as though his hands were touching his chest at times, but in reality he wasn't. That demonstration has always stuck with me, especially when I go beyond the physical realm to see things in the spiritual realm.

At one time in history, the Jews saw Gentiles as nothing more than dogs. The perception of any Gentile was one of disgust. No Gentile person could ever ascend to the level of success of any Jewish person, because in their eyes the Jewish people were God's chosen people. Tradition is tough enough to deal with, not to mention when prejudice jumps

## In the Eye of the Beholder

on the bandwagon, making perception even more skewed. If the Lord were ever to bring salvation to the Gentiles, something dramatic would have to happen in the lives of the Hebrew nation to see things differently.

### A Gentile Prayer Reaches Heaven

As the prayers of Cornelius made their way to the presence of God, it was enough for the Lord to bring the salvation plan to the Gentiles. Without even knowing the one and true God, his dedication to prayer and worship caught the eye of the Lord. That being said, God needed a man to deliver this message and the lot fell upon the apostle Peter. As prejudiced as all get out, it appeared that the Lord had committed an error in trying to convince this servant of God that this precious salvation needed to be sent to a Gentile nation that he himself abhorred his entire life. In a time of consecration, Peter received a vision from God. As a sheet was let down from heaven with four wild beasts, what came next was totally unexpected. Observe the manner in which God attempted to get his attention:

> *And I heard a voice saying to me, 'Rise, Peter; kill and eat.' But I said, 'Not so, Lord! For nothing common or unclean has at any time entered my mouth.' But the voice answered me again from heaven, 'What God has cleansed you must not call common.' Now this was done three times, and all were drawn up again into heaven.* (Acts 11:7-10)

Trying to figure out what he had just seen and experienced, a knock on the door brought him back to reality. The request of the Gentile man he found knocking at the door began to help him make more sense of the vision. As a servant of Cornelius, he had asked Peter to come to Caesarea to preach the gospel. Against his better judgment, Peter followed this servant anyway, humbling himself, and preached the Acts 2:38 message as he was told. As the Holy Ghost fell upon them and they were baptized in water, a whole new way of seeing things was brought to light.

There was still one burning question that needed to be addressed. If they, speaking of the Gentiles, were already clean, then why did Peter have to go and preach salvation to them? This is how God sees with His eyes focused on eternity, not in time. In the eyes of our God, there is no yesterday, today, or tomorrow, because there is no time in eternity. This is where the Scripture used at the beginning of the chapter comes into play.

> ...God, who gives life to the dead and calls those things which do not exist as though they did;
> (Romans 4:17)

The Lord already knows the outcome in any situation, in the life of anybody before it happens, and if He says it's good then it's good. What really happened in Caesarea that day was this: What God had seen in eternity had finally come into man's time to become a reality. Peter was willing to see with the eyes of the eternal beholder (Jesus Christ), resulting in an opportunity for you and me not only to be saved, but with that salvation a promise someday to reign with Him in heaven.

### Seeing How God Sees

Seeing in the manner God does is not such an easy task. It takes some getting used to, especially when our past failures have restricted our growth in Him. This next Bible character truly fits the mold of someone with an extremely low self-esteem. His name is Mephibosheth. The Scriptures tell us he was Jonathan's son (King Saul's grandson). He was raised in the King's Courtyard, but he wasn't the run-of-the-mill royal brat. His handicap limited his mobility and he could not walk on his own. As a baby he was dropped, and physically he never recovered. As most handicapped people are, although he was royalty, it did not stop people from taking advantage of him. From personal experience, I know exactly what he had to confront and it wasn't pretty.

Being made fun of as a little boy recovering from polio was somewhat humbling. Even my first grade teacher initially did not want me in her classroom. In her eyes, I was too different. In those days I wore a body cast under my shirt that extended from just below my armpits down to my waist, all the way around my body. There were wires connected to the body cast that allowed my arms to dangle in front of me. My shoes, of course, were orthopedic, and it looked like if I had stepped off a movie set, one where monsters roamed the area, attempting to wreak havoc in the lives they encountered. There were so many times I felt uncomfortable, but what was I to do? Because children at times can be so blunt in their honesty, they don't realize their words are very hurtful.

In returning back to the life of Mephibosheth, the best of medical care could not help him see himself as more than a dead dog (2 Samuel 9:8). A dog in biblical times was perceived as lazy, being despised and considered the lowest type of vileness. To view oneself as a dog, and a dead dog at that, spoke volumes as to the level of self-esteem in which he lived his life. One day as David returned to the palace without really making it public, he found himself somewhat troubled. The Lord had been talking to him about showing kindness to those in King Saul's household, and for Jonathan's sake a search went on until someone was found.

> Then the king said, "Is there not still someone of the house of Saul, to whom I may show the kindness of God?" (2 Samuel 9:3)

While Mephibosheth floundered in his doldrums, God was speaking to the king about changing the course of this young man's life. Others perhaps did not feel that Mephibosheth deserved any special treatment, but that was not how the king saw things. Crippled or not, this young man was still royalty and he needed to be treated as such.

> Now when Mephibosheth the son of Jonathan, the son of Saul, had come to David, he fell on his face and prostrated himself. Then David said, "Mephibosheth?" And he answered, "Here is your servant!" So David said to him, "Do not fear, for I will surely show you kindness for Jonathan your father's sake, and will restore to you all the land of Saul your grandfather; and you shall eat bread at my table continually." (2 Samuel 9:6-7)

In what initially appeared to be an encounter that had bad written all over it, Mephibosheth would have never been able to envision the kindness shown to him that day. His grandpa, King Saul, had ruined it for the rest of the family. Nevertheless, a king sensitive to the voice of God was able to see through His eyes to be a blessing to someone who had fallen out of grace in the eyes of everyone else. Grace, mercy, and forgiveness, just like beauty, truly are in the eye of the beholder.

# In the Eye of the Beholder

## Through the Eyes of a Mom

It is amazing to me how growing up with a handicap did not affect me as adversely as it did so many other children suffering with the same disease. I have to give a lot of credit to my mom, who was always very positive when she dealt with me. There were times when, nursing me back to health through the exercises the doctors had suggested, she took advantage of the time to instill in me the confidence needed to be successful in whatever I chose to do. In her eyes, I was not handicapped. In her eyes, I was just like everyone else. She went to such great lengths to convey that message that after a while, in my mind it became second nature. When I joined the school band, I never let my handicap stop me from learning how to play the trumpet. Of course, because of a lack of strength in my right hand, I had to play left-handed, which looked a little strange. It only took me a year to become the best trumpet player in the district, and because of the handicap everyone made a greater deal of it than it really was. When it came time to play sports, yes, I was somewhat limited, but on the other hand it never stopped me from joining. I took advantage of the only normal part of my body, my legs, and I turned a negative into the opportunity of a lifetime. It only took me two years to become the best kicker in Southern California, and eventually win a scholarship to continue my football career on the university level. Although I wasn't great in the classroom, my grades were good enough to make several honor rolls. If you were to only look at my accomplishments and not my body, you would have figured that there was nothing wrong with me, physically. I felt I had a pretty good handle on adversity and my various afflictions. My insecurities of how I saw myself did not surface until after I had given my heart to the Lord.

I think in one of my earlier books, I made mention that shaking hands was very unnerving for me. My weak grip caused a lot of apprehension, especially in shaking hands with the ladies in the church. Many a time I would go out of my way to avoid that practice, and I found myself with knots in my stomach because it was such a common way of greeting each other. It was bad enough as a teenager to have to battle so many self-esteem issues on a daily basis, but such is life. With all of the adjustments I had to make in my new life serving God, dealing with my physical disabilities was at times overwhelming.

### Is There Something Wrong with Me?

Because of my lack of understanding of the ways of God, I was constantly in a spiritual fog. Although I had prayed as best I could so that God could heal me, I never had success in that area. I began to question everything. Why wasn't I getting healed? Is there something wrong that I'm doing, is God mad at me for any particular reason? These questions and so many more rattled through my brain constantly and I rarely found myself at peace. It got to the point that questioning my salvation was a constant thorn in the flesh. Why would the Lord go out of His way to save me when I am pretty much useless to Him in this physical condition? I had pretty much hit rock bottom when thoughts of going back on my commitment began to look better and better to me every day. Before I came to know the Lord, this kind of stress was foreign to me. I could always control my destiny in the past by putting my nose to the grindstone and outworking everyone else. I was a classic overachiever, but I was to find out in the spiritual realm hard work at times does not equate to success. With God, timing is everything, and sometimes in my mind He was just too slow.

One of the greatest lessons I learned at that time was never to make a major decision when things are going wrong. As hurtful and stressful as life can be, God never meant for one to stay in the valley of distress. It was ultimately designed for one to pass through to a better place. So many bad decisions have been made hastily with the intentions of relieving the pain experienced at that time. These bad experiences result in more pain and only make matters worse. I almost made one of those decisions when, after two years of not playing football, I received a scholarship offer from Utah State. One of the former coaches on staff at USC had recently taken the head coaching position at Utah State, and he wanted me to follow him as well. Without any kind of tryout, without a visit to the campus, completely sight unseen, he wanted a decision and he wanted it immediately. I came so close to saying yes on the spot, the only thing stopping me was a check in my spirit that was initiated by God.

> *When you pass through the waters, I will be with you; and through the rivers, they shall not overflow you. When you walk through the fire, you shall not be burned, nor shall the flame scorch you. For I am the LORD your God, The Holy One of Israel, your Savior;... Since you were precious in My sight, you have been honored, and I have loved you;*
> 
> (Isaiah 43:2-4)

Oh, how I wanted to believe those words and apply them personally to my life, but I felt it so difficult to do so. Although I still did not comprehend everything God was trying to do in my life, this one thing I was sure of. I was to stay put until God said to move, even though my life was hanging on a string. If I was going to understand God's dealings with me, I was going to have to have a major attitude adjustment. These lingering thoughts of negativity about my physical condition were not doing me any favors. That being said, God decided to call me on the carpet.

### An Experience I'll Never Forget

I decided to attend a youth section service in a neighboring church on a Saturday evening. We are going back to the mid-70s when I was still pretty much a new convert. I really don't remember who the special speaker was, much less the choirs that sang, yet it was one of those services that would impact me for the rest of my life. As the service really got going, and usually youth services are far livelier than regular ones on Sundays, the Spirit of God was being manifested in an unusually powerful manner. I kid you not, from the platform to the last seat in the back of the sanctuary, the blessings of God were falling down on everybody. Everybody, except me! As I tried to find God that day so I too could be a participant in His magnificent glory, I could not make any headway in the Spirit. When I began to plead with God to let me feel what everyone else was feeling, His response to my petition completely blew me away.

He said, "Raise your right arm and worship me."

Immediately my defense mechanisms went out and I responded, "You know that's not possible."

He said it again, "Raise your right arm and worship me."

By this time I was really agitated, because in the past nothing good ever happened when I tried to do what He was asking. Because of a lack of strength and control, I never knew what was going to happen when I raised that arm. At best it trembled and shook, at worst it would fall back down, sometimes hitting me in the face. When He said it a third time, I completely lost it. The tears began to stream down my cheeks and emotionally I was a mess.

I mustered up enough nerve to say this defiantly, "Look at this miserable piece of garbage." I had taken my right arm by the left hand and raised it rebelliously to the sky. "It is frail, ugly, and completely worthless. Why didn't You just heal me completely when You had the chance? You can ask anything of me and I will do it, but please don't ask me to worship You with my right arm raised."

He waited for a while until He saw that I had calmed down. When I did so, He was willing to reveal to me how He actually saw my situation. You see, God has the greatest vantage point to see our lives in Him. Because He is not limited to time and space, living in eternity, His vision is far greater than ours. In my eyes, my physical condition was holding me back. In His eyes, He said it this way to me, "I love you just the way you are."

Never in my entire life had I heard words that were so influential to me. I immediately broke down, completely humbled by His words, and little by little I began to raise my right arm, worshiping His holy name. It was at that time His manifest presence fell upon me, just like everyone else, and I left the sanctuary that day a completely different person.

I don't know if we will ever be able to see things the way He does. Perhaps that time will come when we meet Him in the air. I believe that until that time actually comes, knowing our God sees things differently lets us allow Him to take the lead as to what is good or beautiful or beneficial in our lives. This may sound somewhat ludicrous, blindly following a God who at times does not explain Himself. But I think that we can take that step of faith with all confidence, knowing He sees those things that are not as though they were. Won't you give Him the opportunity to sign, seal, and deliver your blessing today? Remember, beauty is in the eye of the beholder and it is our God whose eyes are upon us.

# CHAPTER 6

## Enjoying Fruit In Your Land of Affliction

*And the name of the second he called Ephraim: "For God has caused me to be fruitful in the land of my affliction."* (Genesis 41:52)

Naming children as a reminder of unforgettable experiences was a common Old Testament practice. Each tribe of Israel had a significant meaning. For instance, Judah means, *may God be praised*. Benjamin means, *son of my right hand*. Some were named at a time that the blessings of God were evident in the life of Jacob. On the other hand, there were tribes named at a time that everything in his life was running amok. As this custom was passed down from generation to generation, the Scripture that we have cited here in Genesis 41 is a good example of what I am talking about.

Joseph was a man who endured more than his share of afflictions. The adverse conditions he had to overcome were not only somewhat numerous, they were excessively painful as well. As the Lord guided him to victory in each and every circumstance, he never failed to give God the glory. That is exactly what he had in mind when he named his two boys Manasseh and Ephraim. Although both names had great significance to Joseph, it is his younger son Ephraim whom we would like to consider. The literal meaning of this son's name was "doubly fruitful."[12] He was named doubly fruitful because even in the land of his affliction, it could not stop God from blessing his father, Joseph. Just about any person can be blessed when things are going well, but to have those same blessings follow you when things in life are going south, that person truly is doubly blessed. These sanctions Joseph received from heaven were powerful enough to produce unmerited blessings.

### An Unmerited Blessing

One such unmerited blessing came in the form of receiving the family birthright. When it came time for Jacob, the family patriarch, to pass along blessings to the next generation, he performed his duty in a very unorthodox way. Joseph's sons had been somewhat adopted by their grandfather, so in essence they too had a part in the blessing ceremony. It would not have been so bad if what happened next would have never occurred. Right before placing his hands on both Manasseh, the elder son, and Ephraim, the younger, he crossed his hands and then proceeded to pronounce the birthright reserved for the eldest son to be given to the younger. As Joseph tried to undo what his father was establishing by the crossing of the hands, Jacob rebuked him and told him he knew what he was doing.

> But his father refused and said, "I know, my son, I know. He also shall become a people, and he also

*shall be great; but truly his younger brother shall be greater than he, and his descendants shall become a multitude of nations."* (Genesis 48:19)

The spiritual implications reached further into the future than anyone could imagine. Although the dispensation of grace was still very much in the distant future, this demonstration of grace would be one of many sprinkled throughout the Scriptures before its time. This unmerited birthright meant that Ephraim would be placed in a close and favored covenant relationship with Jehovah. In other words, that meant God's grace would forever follow him. In the future as his tribe faced adversity, strength and courage could be mustered by the mere mentioning of his name: "God has caused me to be fruitful in the land of my affliction." It was his tribe's destiny to be fruitful in whatever afflictions they would encounter. If they would put their faith to action, God would honor it with innumerable blessings.

### *A Constant Reminder*

We could now take the strength of his name, applying it whenever necessary, when the children of Israel needed a boost in their faith. One such application could be found in the life of Joshua. He, too, had a meaningful name that had a great impact wherever he went. Joshua meant, "Jehovah is salvation."[13] The mentioning of his name would always bring honor unto God. His name proved to be that constant reminder needed to remember Jehovah was the difference in his life. If that wasn't enough, we find that Joshua's tribal affiliation was the tribe of Ephraim. He too originated from the tribe that was destined to be fruitful no matter what.

As he was being groomed to lead Israel after the death of Moses, the first responsibility given to him was charge of the tabernacle.

> *So the LORD spoke to Moses face to face, as a man speaks to his friend. And he would return to the camp, but his servant Joshua the son of Nun, a young man, did not depart from the tabernacle.*
> (Exodus 33:11)

There is something to be said about spending time in the presence of the Lord. It will give you a leg up in your spiritual affairs. In actuality, it is a principle that can be applied to just about any situation where striving for excellence is involved. Two such experiences happened to me in my teen years.

### Dedicating My Time

The reason why I had so much success kicking a football in high school was because I was totally dedicated to it. That meant in the summertime when there was no summer school, I could be found in the gym and on the football field up to thirteen hours a day. I had turned down many an opportunity to go with friends to the beach and just hang out. There were other times while others were going out on a date, becoming very social, I chose to celebrate rarely but grind daily. I thought I had died and gone to heaven when I was allowed to be a student janitor in the summer of my junior year. My main responsibility was to clean the gymnasium, the various workout rooms inside, not to mention the disgustingly smelly weight room. I was as happy as a lark because this job meant I could spend just as much time at school as I had in the past, but actually get paid for it. I took advantage of the situation and spent my time wisely, striving to be the best that I could possibly be. It is little wonder that I was able to set state records that would stand for fifteen years, which brought much attention to me. The scholarship offers came from various schools around the country, and I could pretty much pick where I wanted to go. Of course, it had to be a school with a great athletic program coupled with the academic program I was interested in at the time, which was physical therapy. I finally settled on spending my college football career at the University of Southern California (USC).

The other occurrence in my life that actually could be compared favorably to Joshua's was my time spent as the church janitor. As I look back on it now, I don't know if my prior spirit as a janitor helped me or not but my attitude was the same. It didn't matter that it was a merciless job with no pay, for me I was just delighted I could do anything for God and His kingdom. My responsibilities in cleaning the church may not have been as dynamic as those given to Joshua, but like him, it gave me significant time to spend in the presence of the Lord. To make the time pass more efficiently, I would hold mock services, praising the night away, feeling His Shekinah glory as my praises went up as a sweet smelling savor. It was in those early days, still trying to figure out what God wanted in my life, that I constantly found myself alone with Him, seeking His face. As I have grown in His grace, there are many who have asked how the Gifts of the Spirit had come to flourish so powerfully in my ministry. It is usually followed by this question: "How can I obtain a powerful anointing like you so that the Gifts of the Spirit might flow freely in my life?" For me, that has always been an easy question to answer. Although many times others have been disillusioned by my response, it is still the only way I know to get to that level. The answer can be found in the Scripture below:

> *When You said, "Seek My face," My heart said to You, "Your face, LORD, I will seek."* (Psalms 27:8)

I will admonish anyone who will listen to stop seeking His gifts and instead seek His face. When you have established a personal relationship with our Lord and you can be trusted, the revelations hidden for His chosen vessels will be revealed unto you. Attempting any other way is nothing more than spinning your wheels and wishful thinking.

### The Church of Today

The Church of today would be doing really good to follow Joshua's lead. Yet if you need a New Testament reference to confirm my words, here's one:

> *"I am the vine, you are the branches. He who abides in Me, and I in him, bears much fruit; for without Me you can do nothing*
>
> (John 15:5)

Because abiding in Him will take an enormous amount of time, abiding in today's Christian world is a lost art. Our efforts to accomplish His will never initially include Him, because our faith in technology makes us look better than we really are. Then when our assignments fail miserably, He is the one to get the blame. If there were ever any words Christ had left for us to remember, it would be that last phrase in the Scripture above. We must bear in mind that without Him, we can do nothing.

Another false assumption we make is that if we do take the time to abide in God alone, it will negate the afflictions of life. That cannot be further from the truth. As Joshua exited the tabernacle, spiritually ready for his next assignment, he was not immune from criticism or ridicule. Moses had chosen him along with eleven others to spy out Canaan land. It should have been an easy assignment because all they were asked to do was to come back, reporting ahead of time the blessings they would find once they conquered the land. It did not turn out anything like that. The only constructive thing that came out of that fiasco was the godly influence Joshua had on Caleb. This converted Jew was the only one to back him up when the rest of the spies opposed him. Joshua's sin, in their eyes, was the fact that he believed God was powerful enough to overcome the giants in the land. For this show of faith, the spies wanted to kill him by stoning him to death.

### *Reveling in Their Affliction*

Giants in the land did not scare Joshua because his tribe reveled in their affliction, which is exactly where the fruit was. If it were only physical afflictions he had to deal with, it would have made his life so much easier. But the fact of the matter is that if you are to be considered doubly fruitful, then sure as you're born satan will attack you with double the afflictions. That is where the afflictions of the mind come in. It is extremely demanding to complete your assignment when the rejection you are receiving is when you are right. It is bad enough dealing with rejection when you're wrong, but having to deal with it when you have been right cuts deeper and hurts even more. These afflictions like daggers come from all directions with such intensity that they are difficult to fight off emotionally. You might have to stand alone with only your integrity backing you up. If that be so, it will be enough.

> *Vindicate me, O LORD, For I have walked in my integrity. I have also trusted in the LORD; I shall not slip.* (Psalms 26:1)

A definite decision must be made to hang on tightly to the Lord, trusting in Him that you might not lose your integrity. Once that integrity is lost, it will never be recovered and your accomplishments will dwindle down to nothing.

For their disobedience, God judged Israel and they were then forced to wander in the wilderness until all of the rebellious, unbelieving people were dead. After forty years of affliction, Moses died and Joshua was placed as the new leader. It was time to set things in order by the restoring of tribal heritages. There was a new generation of Hebrews who did not know what their tribes stood for, so Joshua and Caleb would be the only remnant they would have to seek for guidance.

### Building Faith at Jericho

If they were to be successful in this endeavor, their faith had to be built up, which meant the conquering of Canaan would begin in Jericho. You could have not asked for a tougher assignment because the inhabitants of Jericho were expert warriors, experienced in the art of war. To increase the difficulty of overthrowing Jericho, their fortified city walls were impenetrable. History tells us the walls were at least twelve to seventeen feet high and approximately five feet wide.[14]

The first order of business included instilling pride in their new recruits by teaching them the meaning of

Ephraim. "Doubly fruitful" would become their daily mantra. The extension of the blessing could find its way through the most severe afflictions they would be asked to endure. It all meant nothing if they were not willing to put their faith to work. That moment came when their marching orders included crazy ones that did not make any sense at all. They were instructed to march around the city walls once a day for six days in utter silence. On the seventh day, it was to be done seven times. After doing so, the priests would make their way to the front, and when Joshua gave the instruction, in unison they would blow their trumpets. When the army heard the sound of these instruments, a shout of victory was to be made before the fact. It was this shout of praise that brought down the impenetrable walls of Jericho.

Only a moron would believe that without lifting a finger, one of the greatest fortified cities in the world could be destroyed.

*But Jesus looked at them and said, "With men it is impossible, but not with God; for with God all things are possible."* (Mark 10:27)

Is it any wonder that at another time, the Lord declared that if we did not become as little children, we would not be able to enter into the kingdom of heaven? It takes a childlike faith to believe God for the impossible. With the destruction of the walls staring them in the face, these new, inexperienced Israeli warriors found their faith and morale skyrocketing to gigantic proportions. If God could annihilate their most feared foe with such ease, can you imagine what He could do to the rest of their enemies in Canaan? The onslaught to conquer Canaan continued until it came time to divide the inheritance amongst the different tribes.

### A Crazy Old Man

It was at this point in Scripture that Caleb came back into the picture. He emotionally pled with Joshua to give him Hebron, the land of the giants.

> *As yet I am as strong this day as on the day that Moses sent me; just as my strength was then, so now is my strength for war, both for going out and for coming in. Now therefore, give me this mountain of which the LORD spoke in that day; for you heard in that day how the Anakim were there, and that the cities were great and fortified. It may be that the LORD will be with me, and I shall be able to drive them out as the LORD said."* (Joshua 14:11-12)

What audacity! Not only was he now eighty-five years old and pretty much over the hill, it appeared he was also living in the past. He had to be considered completely delusional if he honestly believed his own words. To add insult to injury, he was not even a native born Jew. Only through special considerations in the word allowing a Gentile to become a follower of Jehovah was he able to have anything to do with the Jewish nation. Once he was circumcised, he had his pick of the litter, meaning whichever tribe of Israel appealed to him most, that would be the one he could choose. He ended up settling on the tribe of Judah, one that was famous in their praising of God. Later in life, this decision would prove to have been a great choice because he would have to use its reputation to help him out of an impossible situation. In truth, his moxie came from Joshua himself. It was Joshua's courage in times of affliction that rubbed off on this grafted in Hebrew, believing his newfound God for the impossible. If the inheritance he was asking for was to be obtained, it would have to be obtained the same way Ephraim obtained his birthright, with unmerited favor. Considering he was not born into God's people of promise, the Lord chose him anyway before Caleb even knew there was a God by the name of Jehovah. God choosing him ahead of time made all the difference in the world. That meant grace had fallen upon him and he was destined to bear fruit. Isn't that just the way it happened with us?

> *You did not choose Me, but I chose you and appointed you that you should go and bear fruit, and that your fruit should remain, that whatever you ask the Father in My name He may give you.*
> (John 15:16)

Today we are part of this kingdom of God, being grafted in by His grace, and we too are destined to be fruitful.

### True or False?

As we take some time to revisit Caleb's outrageous statement, we find that it is both true and false. It was false in the sense that physically he really did not have the same strength in his body that was prevalent forty-five years ago. What was true about his statement was the fact that the source of his strength had not changed. His wise choice in choosing the tribe of Judah allowed him the luxury to become a great man of praise and an excellent worshiper of Jehovah. That is where he drew his strength.

Caleb had come a long way from those early days of spying out Canaan. What had helped him become a great man of God was the fact that he was willing to incorporate the strengths of the tribe of Ephraim with the strength of the tribe of Judah. He knew from the outset that he would bear fruit in both good times and bad times, and that the worst of afflictions would never stop the floodgates of heaven from blessing his life. With that knowledge, he praised God all the day long. This proved to be a recipe of disaster for the hated Anakim. Their giant stature would not intimidate this man of God, and knowing that their greatest weapon had been defused they were no match for Caleb and his mighty warriors. I believe David had this in mind when he sat down one day to write this in one of his Psalms:

> *I will call upon the LORD, who is worthy to be praised; So shall I be saved from my enemies.*
> (Psalms 18:3)

Praising God in your land of affliction will always defeat the giants in your life.

### A Great Lesson to Be Learned

The greatest lesson to be learned from the experiences of these two great men of God is that in times of great affliction, God does not wipe away His promises of fruitfulness. Too many Christians of today live their lives in an "either or" state. By that I mean their lives are either in a place of all blessing or all affliction. They do not leave room for the blessings of God to fall upon them at the same time the afflictions of life are bogging them down. Our lives in God should not be perceived as an up and down experience. We should rather see blessing and affliction run concurrently side-by-side. Another thing that must be taken into consideration is the fact that our blessings are not solely dependent on the sovereignty of God. We have taken waiting upon God to an extreme when His grace at times will travel at a snail's pace. We mustn't be afraid to take the initiative to make His promises to us come to life. That is the reason why God has established our sacrifice of praise as an instrument we can use to secure an answer.

> *Therefore by Him let us continually offer the sacrifice of praise to God, that is, the fruit of our lips, giving thanks to His name.* (Hebrews 13:15)

By continually offering a sacrifice of praise unto God, it was meant for us to see that God is allowing us to participate in the blessing He has promised.

It boils down once again to our attitude. I know this has been mentioned in prior chapters. Needless to say, it bears repeating because of its importance in our receiving of the best God has to offer. Don't be pigheaded like Naaman. When his servant came back with instructions from the man of God as to how he would obtain his healing, Naaman was offended by what he heard. Was it really that difficult to bathe himself in the Jordan River? Yeah, yeah, I know it was the filthiest river in the land. But on the other hand, if it were to be the only way to rid him of this dreaded leprosy, humbling himself to do it would turn out to be his most difficult task. If humbling yourself to be blessed of God is the only thing holding you back from being set free, I believe you should rethink your position. If you need any kind of nudge or inspiration, look at this Psalm:

> *From the rising of the sun to its going down the LORD's name is to be praised.* (Psalms 113:3)

Down through the history of time, no one seems to know who wrote this particular Psalm. It might as well be you! Let this Psalm become a personal motivator, one that will become a daily tune, helping you accept and enjoy fruit, especially in your land of affliction. If that doesn't do the trick, then take to heart the definition of Ephraim and let it penetrate to the deepest depths of your soul. You will begin to believe God for the impossible in the most difficult of times, and if you are successful in this assignment, there will always be fruit in the land of your affliction.

# CHAPTER 7

## The Tenderness of a Woman

*And be kind to one another, tenderhearted, forgiving one another, even as God in Christ forgave you.* (Ephesians 4:32)

In all of the books I have written in the past (this is my fourth), there has been at least one chapter titled in such a way that gave an impression I had strayed away from the subject matter. Many a reader has been somewhat puzzled when thumbing over to the table of contents, only to find a title that appeared out of place. You have come to that chapter in this book. If you are like a lot of folks who try to figure out ahead of time what direction an author is going when writing, then you'll be sadly disappointed when it turns out nothing like you thought.

It would be easy to assume the words forgiving and/or forgiveness would be the focus of the chapter. In some ways it is, and in other ways it's not. Tenderhearted is the word that is the key to this chapter. As you go along with me on this journey, especially if you are a woman, at the outset you will have issues with what I write. You will not like what I have written, believing my point of view is male chauvinist. Again, when the Lord initially gave me this message, it wasn't with the intention of women bashing. The Lord placed it in my heart that it could be used as a warning to the ladies of this generation who have lost their tenderness, one that was placed there in the beginning by God Himself. What does that loss have to do with a book focused on afflictions? You are about to see! Let me digress a bit and give you some definitions that will help set the foundation for this little talk. Webster took a great amount of time to leave quite a few definitions of the word tender. It can be found written as an adjective, noun, or verb with at least thirty-one definitions in all.[15]

Being tender can be a strength in your life, or it can prove to be a great weakness. Because all of the definitions do not apply to this subject, I chose the following ones to make a point. On the positive side, a tender person is one who shows care and is considerate. They are sensitive to touch or palpitation.[16] Although this word does not fall under the category of one of the fruits of the Spirit, it surely could have qualified. As a person tenderly shows with loving care consideration for others, they are essentially following the golden rule. Leading the way at the pole position, the golden rule sits head and shoulders above many of God's other more famous commandments, (i.e., the Ten Commandments). It will look hypocrisy in the face, nip it in the bud, and be used as a gauge to measure our intentions.

> *Therefore, whatever you want men to do to you, do also to them, for this is the Law and the Prophets.*
> *(Matthew 7:12)*

Likewise, a tenderhearted person is sensitive to the voice of God. God's heartbeat becomes their heartbeat and it is much easier to follow His instructions because of their intimate relationship with the Master.

## *A Misunderstood Definition*

As wonderful as the first part of the definition sounds, a completely different world opens up when accepting the more pessimistic definition of tender, believing it to be the one and only way it should be perceived. Webster went on to define tender as being physically weak and immature. This tender person would not be able to endure hardship (see Chapter 4) and would be highly susceptible to emotions, especially damaging ones. He went on to define tender as being highly sensitive to injury or insults, becoming touchy.[17] As you can see, these undesirable definitions as such are more detrimental to a person's character than the positive definitions are beneficial.

In generations past, tenderness was considered an inborn characteristic for a woman. Her tender and gentle ways would burst out naturally, causing us to conclude this was the characteristic God placed in her to distinguish the difference between male and female. I have purposely written that this train of thought was one accepted in past generations, because in the times that we live today it is no longer the status quo. There are many reasons for this paradigm shift, but the one reason I believe is the cause of this upheaval in mindset amongst our women is because of the abuse they have had to bear by way of the men in their lives. The afflictions have been too many and too great.

It is true that in the beginning, God placed man in authority over the entire Earth. This license to govern included his future wife and family. Sadly to say, we as mankind have not done such a great job with the authority that has been placed in our hands. It has been much easier to demand things of our families, especially our wives, and not be held to the same standard. Whenever we have been challenged in the past, (mankind) we have shamefully hid behind the word of God, misquoting and misinterpreting the Scriptures so they could be manipulated to our advantage. These abuses (mental, physical, emotional, and verbal) have been so damaging that the psyche of our women has been marred beyond repair. They are no longer willing to sit quietly in despair, waiting for the next abuse to find its mark. With the help of a radical change in our society back in the 90s, the Christian woman has decided to fight similar to the way a woman who does not know God does.

### A Hidden Agenda

When the women's liberation movement began back in the 70s, no one could honestly predict in the future how our families were to be affected. Behind the guise of "equal pay for equal work," the hidden agenda took years to finally come to the surface. What started out as a logical, sensible, nonthreatening way to balance the inequities between men and women turned out to be the beginning of our downfall in this country. Although the experience I'm about to write has nothing to do with the conflict between men and women, it broadens the scope of the adverse effect this change in mindset has had not only on our society, but for future generations as well.

I had some free time to spend and I walked across the street to the park near our home. A girls' softball team was playing, and whether it is boys or girls, if it is good competition I'll watch. As I stood behind the backstop, observing the talent of the young lady pitching that day, the voice of the Lord instructed me to take notice of the young lady at bat. Initially in trying to figure out what lesson the Lord was trying to teach me, it was going completely over my head. I began to study closer her movements and I found out that she was mimicking many of the rituals she had seen her male counterparts do in their games. The way she moved her bat, dug her cleats into the dirt, and spat when she stepped out of the batter's box; it was all very masculine and unfeminine. I learned that day that although playing sports for girls is not necessarily a sin, if care is not taken in the attitudes and mannerisms of that sport, these young ladies will fall into the trap of "doing it like the guys," and in the process lose their femininity as well.

From the beginning of time, the Lord has not wavered in His demand for a distinction between male and female. Whether in dress or actions, this law in His kingdom, if broken, would not be tolerated by Him. It would be categorized as an abomination (Deuteronomy 22:5). Why would we ever want to be found guilty of doing something the Lord hates? The fact that this practice has become commonplace in our society does not make it right. What makes it even more distressing is the fact that this same spirit has crept into the church, and the spiritual repercussions are ones that we will be heavily judged for. Now, let us go back to the tenderness of a woman and see how its importance has been thrown out with the bath water, being replaced by something in the lives of women that will ultimately prove disastrous.

### *God's Feminine Side?*

In the beginning, God had placed tenderness in the woman because it was a part of Him He wanted to share with all mankind. From Scripture, we can see that the Lord has always shown this mercy because it is mentioned in His word 282 times. What makes His mercy even more effective is the fact that twelve times that same word mercy is described as "tender mercies." You could say His tender mercies are nothing more than His soft side (His feminine side?). From the outset He has been sensitive, sympathetic, understanding, warm, and loving. In other words, He is everything the natural man isn't! I placed a question mark on the words feminine side because most males reading this have a difficult time believing that their God is soft in any way. Depending on the culture, men in general have tried to suppress these gentle characteristics of God in their lives because they don't want to see Jesus as lowly, meek, or gentle. That effeminate stuff should be reserved for women and women only, because according to Scripture they (women), not us, are the weaker vessel. With a mentality like that, is it any wonder why prayers are being hindered?

> *Husbands, likewise, dwell with them with understanding, giving honor to the wife, as to the weaker vessel, and as being heirs together of the grace of life, that your prayers may not be hindered.*
> (1 Peter 3:7)

If the tender side of God is so vital to be successful in this world, then why wasn't it put in man from the beginning? If Christ has demonstrated that particular trait throughout eternity, then where is it now? God in His infinite wisdom knew in the future His creation, man, would not readily accept the tender side of God, so He did the next best thing. He put Adam to sleep, opened up his side, taking a rib and tenderness with it, and He placed it in the woman. She was created out of necessity because Adam needed a helper in all he was doing in the Garden of

Eden, one that would be comparable to him (Genesis 2:18). The word comparable in the Scripture literally means counterpart -- a person who completes another.[18] She was not created as the animals were (i.e., from the ground); she was created directly from a rib in Adam's chest.

*And the LORD God caused a deep sleep to fall on Adam, and he slept; and He took one of his ribs, and closed up the flesh in its place. Then the rib which the LORD God had taken from man He made into a woman, and He brought her to the man. And Adam said: "This is now bone of my bones and flesh of my flesh; she shall be called Woman, because she was taken out of Man."* (Genesis 2:21-23)

All of the tender characteristics in God that helped form his fullness were taken out of Adam and were placed in his wife. When God finished the creating process, He did something that very few people are aware of. He took His dominant qualities He placed in man (power, authority, anointing, etc.). He then mixed them with His tender qualities (patience, kindness, gentleness, etc.) to form the fullness of God on earth. When He saw that all was good, He decided to name them both, Adam.

*Male and female created he them; and blessed them, and called their name Adam, in the day when they were created.* (Gen 5:2 KJV)

## *God's Original Plan*

The original plan in creation after the woman was formed was that man and woman would rule together equally. Giving them the same name would make it easier on Adam to accept the woman God had given him to be his counterpart, yet she was given a different set of characteristics that would prove her worth here on earth. It wasn't until Adam II (the woman) sinned that God placed the woman under the authority of her husband.

> *To the woman He said: "I will greatly multiply your sorrow and your conception; In pain you shall bring forth children; your desire shall be for your husband, and he shall rule over you."*
> (Genesis 3:16)

After the passing out of judgment was complete and they were thrown out of the Garden of Eden, the name of the woman we all recognize, Eve, was then given to her by Adam

> *And Adam called his wife's name Eve, because she was the mother of all living.* (Genesis 3:20)

Now it becomes clearer why there is so much hostility in wives when they are told they must submit to the authority of their husbands. A judgment, like a jail sentence, is not a delightful experience. An inmate has few rights, if any, and is usually treated without much respect. Their opinions have no weight, and at best they are treated like second-class citizens. The complaints of this type of treatment by women have gone on for such an extended period of time that finally this mistreatment has caused our women to snap. Herein lies the problem.

When the creation plan began to unfold, it was God's intention for the woman to be an integral part of expanding His glory beyond their lifetimes. With the man taking authoritative charge of the adversities in life, coupled with the woman tenderly becoming that calming voice, together

## The Tenderness of a Woman

they could provide the world with a perfect example of who God was.

### A Decision Gone Bad

As time moved on, the woman's advantage in this area began to be whittled away. The tenderness of God placed in the woman meant nothing to her because, all it got her was an enormous amount of grief. In trying to remedy the situation and bring equality to the sexes, women made a decision that would in the long run prove to be destructive. These confrontations with the opposite sex would be fought on their (women's) turf, meaning their choice of battle strategies would be similar to those of their male counterparts. In other words, they would fight like men. This would be no problem, because for generations now women have started to mimic men in other areas of life. I've already mentioned above one of the areas "copycatted" by our women, the sports world. Sad to say, it hasn't stopped there. This mindset has filtered down into areas of business, education, the military and even religion. The dam has burst and there's no going back.

Is what I have written really as horrendous as I have portrayed it to be? Most would say my opinions have a bent towards being narrow-minded and dogmatic, but I would not be offended if that point of view were to be taken. So what if our young ladies are taking on masculine traits in the sports world? Big deal. As far as business is concerned, there are occasions a woman's business savvy far exceeds that of a man. Many would say there's nothing wrong with women taking the battlefield in the military as well. If that's what they want, more power to them. In religion, as far as a woman taking a pulpit, anyone refusing her that right really isn't in tune with God and the Scriptures. But someone must be able to see beyond the self-serving decisions women have made that will overturn the will of God for the generations who follow in our footsteps.

### A Three-Fold Loss

Let me reel this whopper in and let me get down to brass tacks. The losses that will occur, if women are allowed to continue in the ways they have chosen, will unfold in three different areas. First of all, when a woman chooses to leave her tender feminine side to fight her battles as a man, the first casualty in this confrontation is the man himself. Where else can a man find the tender attributes besides those given to women? If she abandons them completely, he will have to assume that because he was created in the image of God, then the Lord would deal with him the way he deals with others, usually very harshly. How many times has a wife been able to calm down her husband with soothing, comforting, gentle, and relaxing words? Picture if you will a man coming to his wife, and without her being that counterbalance, counseling him to react the way she would (without tenderness). Her counsel would always be skewed to the harsh side of life and he would never be as successful without a different point of view. That is what has begun to happen in our homes today.

The second loss would involve the woman herself. Vacating her purpose in life would be more hurtful than what we can visually see. I would imagine as a woman the "unsung hero" label only goes so far. When you are underappreciated, undervalued, and taken for granted, it makes it extremely difficult to believe that your purpose in life has any value whatsoever. Women must not forget that God placed them in this position because in many ways they were stronger than their partner. Isn't it a mother whom God will usually commission to intercede for wayward children? Wasn't it a woman God had chosen for childbearing, knowing that no way in the world would a man be able to withstand so much pain? The adverse treatment and the great afflictions have not been allowed in a woman's life to destroy her (although the enemy would like her to believe that). Like the confidence God showed in Job as He bragged to the devil about His servant, so does the Lord have confidence in woman that she too will not let Him down. It is God's delight to brag on His feminine creation. In essence, God knows that a woman has the capacity to withstand the greatest adversities life can present.

The final loss, the greatest loss of all, would have to include our children. They have been placed in our care so as pliable clay their lives could be molded to be pleasing to God. Sad to say, this generation more so than others in the past has grown up confused. They are confused in the sense that there is no longer a clear-cut distinction between man and woman. Even though their parents do dress somewhat different, it's not the kind of a distinction needed to put their minds at ease. This is the case especially in one-parent households where the mother is the only parent present. Because she has been forced into playing a double role, the man's role of authority surfaces more frequently and Mama's tender side is put on the back burner. The result is that Junior has no buffer to console him when Mom has been harsh, and if this continues many times he will grow up hating women in general, and when it comes time to find a partner to love, he will search for companionship in his own sex.

Can I go a little bit deeper with this? I know it is possible for a mother to raise her children alone without the help of a man in the household and still raise balanced children. If that is to be the case, a mother's dedication to her God must be paramount. As she seeks the face of the Lord, it must be sought with the doggedness of a man yet with the tenderness of a woman. Her prayer life must take priority in the everyday functions of life, and if so she will obtain the wisdom necessary to lead her children down the right pathway. I have written these words from personal experience.

My mom was such a woman. Her dedication to prayer was passed on to her by her mother (see chapter 4). And even though she was a backslider when her divorce to my father was final, the example set over the years by my grandmother was never forgotten.

*Train up a child in the way he should go, and when he is old he will not depart from it.* (Proverbs 22:6)

It was never her choice to be placed in this position of authority, but out of necessity she buckled up her seat belt, called on the name of the Lord, and prepared herself for the ride of her life. Through every adverse situation she encountered, no matter how severe the afflictions became, she never once lost sight of her tender loving ways. With God's help, and none from my father, she was able to make a great comeback and balance things out. You could see the pride in her face every time she could say that all three of her children had committed their lives to Christ.

### *It Will Only Get Worse*

Back to the losses to be endured as the chain of command becomes more blurred. It only gets worse! Read with me the ugly warning the apostle Paul left for Timothy as he prophesied a gloomy future:

## The Tenderness of a Woman

> *For men will be lovers of themselves, lovers of money, boasters, proud, blasphemers, disobedient to parents, unthankful, unholy, unloving, unforgiving, slanderers, without self-control, brutal, despisers of good, traitors, headstrong, haughty, lovers of pleasure rather than lovers of God, having a form of godliness but denying its power. And from such people turn away! For of this sort are those who creep into households and make captives of gullible women loaded down with sins, led away by various lusts, always learning and never able to come to the knowledge of the truth.*
>
> (2 Timothy 3:2-7)

It would take more than a chapter to do justice explaining this portion of Scripture, but I can say this. The undesirable, damaging, pessimistic adjectives used to describe a future generation are certainly ones that can be applied to the days we live in today. What makes it even more depressing is the fact these are church folk we are talking about, *having a form of godliness but denying its power (vs 5)*. It is a generation that has been raised without any tenderness whatsoever, and the result is a world gone mad. It is a generation that is very difficult to reach because tenderness has been taught to them as a weakness, and if that be so, they don't need that kind of God. If they are lucky enough to find their way to salvation, the image of Christ that should be every Christian's goal will be without question out of their reach because there is no example in their lives of those Christ-like characteristics so important in living for Him. They may be saved in principle, but they never embrace the Christian life. That is the reason the apostle steadfastly warns us in verse five: *And from such people turn away!*

The Scripture quoted at the beginning of the chapter has an origin directing itself to men. It would be absurd to believe Paul's admonition was directed to women when they by nature were already tenderhearted. It was a call to unity of sorts, trying to bring the Ephesians together by using one of the more formidable means known in Scripture, that being forgiveness. In Paul's mind, this was doable because first of all they could relate to the forgiveness Christ had had for them. But even more so on a daily basis, man could use the women in his life as examples of how this could be grafted into his life as well. If forgiveness was given the opportunity to bring about that unity, the apostle Paul understood it would have to come through a tender heart.

### A Sad Admittance

In today's world, sad to say, women must be included in the apostle's reprimand in Ephesians chapter 4. Hopefully it's not too late to reverse the damage already done. The only reference point left for either man or woman, as far as tenderness is concerned, is the forgiveness bestowed upon them by God when they were saved. His tender mercies were more than adequate to bring salvation to their lives that certainly were unworthy. If women can embrace the tenderness of God again, the future looks bright. If each one could take their rightful place in God's order and return to His original plan where Adam and Eve had become one flesh, then God can release His glory to bless His people. The fullness of God reigned in that era, why is that not possible now? Spiritually speaking, we can become Adam and Adam II to leave our children and a lost world a presentation of God the way it was meant to be. All it will take is finding the tenderness lost and allowing God to take care of the rest.

# CHAPTER 8

## He Heard my Cry

*In my distress I called upon the LORD, and cried out to my God; He heard my voice from His temple, and my cry entered His ears.* (2 Samuel 22:7)

Asking for help is either something that most of us do not like to do because it makes us uncomfortable or we're just not used to it. When desperation sets in and asking for help becomes more of a cry for help, we find ourselves in uncharted waters. When a literal crying becomes part of our petition, it is then we feel our lives are coming apart at the seams. Although women are more prone to use crying as a method of coping in their distress, many times out of embarrassment they will cry to themselves. They would not like to be seen having such a show of emotion in public. On the other hand, men are even worse. Showing any kind of emotion in public is grounds to have your "man card" revoked. As pride rears its ugly head, almost under no circumstances will a man be caught crying in front of others.

What does it actually mean to cry out? It is nothing more than hollering to attract attention, shouting at the top of your lungs.[19] When desperation begins to mount up, it will usually include tears. I believe that crying out is used as a last resort, because hollering is usually reserved for undesirable situations like arguing or fighting. We can include the use of hollering when we are in disagreement or find ourselves mocking others. The consensus then is the use of hollering becomes more needful when a situation arises where you have completely lost it, and as a result have stepped out of control. Because it contains so much negative energy, it's hard to believe that it could be used for any good.

### How God Sees Crying

The Lord sees things so differently than we do that in His eyes crying out will benefit us immensely. First of all, it is a humbling experience. It goes against our nature to humble ourselves in any way, yet humbling oneself unlocks the gate of blessing in God's kingdom.

> *Humble yourselves in the sight of the Lord, and He will lift you up.* (James 4:10)

There is a promise in this Scripture above that cannot be ignored. As clear and simple as it has been written, putting it into practice is another story. We must be willing to admit that we cannot prevail in this position of need without Him intervening, therefore it is necessary to cry out for His help. This in turn will disarm one of Satan's greatest weapons, pride. The same element used to create his downfall is the same weapon he uses now to misguide others into losing out with God. Humbling ourselves before the throne of God will not only help redeem what satan has stolen, but we will also be exalted by God for our efforts.

> *Therefore humble yourselves under the mighty hand of God, that He may exalt you in due time, casting all your care upon Him, for He cares for you.*
> (1 Peter 5:6-7)

This all-out effort to place ourselves under the mighty hand of God allows a peace to envelop our minds, thus making it easier to leave everything in His hands.

There is another reason God uses a crying out to Him for our benefit. It will guarantee that your petition will be heard. Although the Lord is not deaf, and He even knows what we are going to say before it comes out of our mouth, it's not so much the loudness of our cry that makes Him respond to our need. It is rather the intensity of our exertion that catches His attention. It then has the ability to be heard from the Temple all the way to the throne of heaven, right where it needs to be in His ears.

### *The Lord's Example to Us*

The Lord Himself left us a great example of what a crying out could do. He had been completely broken over the death of His best friend, Lazarus, and when He entered into the city, He found His way to Lazarus' home to offer His condolences to his sisters, Mary and Martha. Certainly He was broken emotionally on the inside but very much composed on the outside. What came next was not totally unexpected, but the degree of the Lord's emotion was certainly more passionate than anticipated. While ministering unto Mary, her tearful emotion-filled cries moved Him deeply, causing Him to groan in His spirit, and He too began to weep.

> *Therefore, when Jesus saw her weeping, and the Jews who came with her weeping, He groaned in the spirit and was troubled. And He said, "Where have you laid him?" They said to Him, "Lord, come and see." Jesus wept.* (John 11:33-35)

With His composure back intact, He offered a simple prayer that produced miraculous results. A loud cry followed that prayer, and look at the outcome.

> *Now when He had said these things, He cried with a loud voice, "Lazarus, come forth!" And he who had died came out bound hand and foot with grave clothes, and his face was wrapped with a cloth. Jesus said to them, "Loose him, and let him go."*
> (John 11:43-44)

That cry caused nature to be reversed and death was turned into life. Better yet, freedom from bondage was unwrapped and he was loosed completely to sing the praises of his God. When we make the concerted effort to cry out onto God, we will have the same result.

### A Crying Out in El Paso

Several years ago, I was ministering in the El Paso area and I came across a situation that I would like to share. When a mother asked me to pray for her son, it was a request that I had never received before. This six-year-old young man could not speak. I found out later the details of his handicap when I later spoke to the mother in private. She said her son had been born premature and weighed less than four pounds at the age of six months. When at two years old he still was not talking, she had his hearing checked and doctors confirmed there was nothing wrong with his hearing. It was later found out that his vocal cords had never been fully developed, and consequently his inability to talk. The doctor's prognosis was that he would never be able to talk and suggested to his mother that he learn to communicate by sign language. Her commitment to him was unrelenting, and she was determined to take whatever recourse necessary to make her child's life as normal as possible. There is nothing like a mother's grit and resolve used to catapult her child's life to a better place. With that in mind, she enrolled him in a regular school without a special education program. This decision would ultimately prove disastrous because of the gawking and teasing her boy would have to endure.

When my mom was put in a similar situation, this quiet woman would not allow the teacher I was assigned to, to refuse to teach me because of my handicap. Being fit to be tied, she stormed into the principal's office, stepping out of character, and blasted him with both barrels. He never saw this coming and certainly did not know what hit him. Of course she, my teacher, was required to apologize and we never had problems with the school itself. That did not stop students from teasing and taunting me. There was a nickname given to me that I never appreciated. I was known to many students as "finger." The fact that the fingers on my right hand at times were uncontrollable, it looked to them like I was giving them the middle finger. They would take their turns asking to see my lifeless hand, and in doing so they would laugh me to scorn saying, "Oh my God, he's giving us the middle finger," and left, laughing almost to the point of tears.

It was at a similar point in this little boy's life that his mom came to me, not only distraught but in desperation. She had found out at school that the kids would mimic the various sounds her child would make when trying to communicate. They saw him as somewhat of a monster, perhaps even an animal, and they took every opportunity possible to make him the brunt of all of their rude and ill-mannered jokes. She would do anything to bring peace to her little boy's life, and she was in essence asking God for a miracle.

### The Pressure Continued to Build

The pressure had slowly been building and it was hitting her from different directions. Not only did she have to put up with what the kids were doing, the school was asking her son to pass an exam that would allow him to stay in public school. If that exam were to be failed, they would have no choice but to put him in a special school. At times that did not seem as such a bad idea, but her son would not have any of it. He wanted to stay at all costs, with his greatest desire being having the ability to talk like everyone else.

I must admit, when I am placed in similar situations where people have become desperate, although I am not the one performing the miracle, it still puts a lot of pressure on me. I feel that I have been called to this ministry because of the afflictions that I have endured in my life. Because of that, I have become more sensitive to the needs of others and my sympathy actually becomes more empathy than anything else. When I laid my hands on this little one, I was so disappointed that after the prayer nothing had changed. His form of communication was still the same, and I not only felt badly for him, but for his mother as well. I ended the revival that day somewhat broken. I began to blame myself for not being able to be a part of the blessing this family had believed God for. I learned that day that God does not need a public platform to perform miracles.

### One Last Cry

The following day would be a judgment day of sorts. The exam was to be taken, nothing had changed in the way of his speaking, and all hope was lost. Completely broken over his plight, the young man began to cry out onto God. As he lay in bed at night, the tears began to stream down his cheeks, and in his own little way he cried out onto his God. He had cried so incessantly long that he cried himself to sleep.

It was at that moment the glory of God found its way into his bedroom. God had heard his cry and had stepped into his life to do something about it. While he slept peacefully, the Lord began to operate as angels stood around applauding His greatness and giving Him glory. When the boy woke up the next morning, the unimaginable had happened. As the Lord touched his body, fully forming his vocal cords, he woke up talking like any other kid. As the rest of the family caught wind of what had happened, the tears of joy ran down their cheeks as if a dam had burst. They knew it was their God who had responded, and not any therapy or medications offered by man. Later that day, mama proudly took her son to school, he sat down and took his exam, and he passed with flying colors.

About a year or so later, I found myself returning to that particular church, and after one of the services I noticed a rambunctious little guy running all over the church, excitedly raising his voice in unabated chatter. When I inquired who this happy-go-lucky kid was, the pastor gleefully responded, "It's the little boy God healed the last time you were here." I could not believe I was gazing at the same young man who, just a year ago, could not form even a word. Like an automatic weapon, he was firing verbal bullets with such clarity you would have never known at one time he could not speak. God sure knows how to respond to the cry of His people.

Was the severity of his mother's afflictions needful for her to cry out onto God? Not really. The fact that this situation lingered as long as it did was because the uneasiness of it all had not reached a level of despondency. The answer was waiting all along, but because crying out onto God was used as a final option, everything was put on hold.

### Living in Desperation

As we live our lives in a world dominated by stress, there are many who have actually fallen into distress. When a person finds himself in distress, it is a painful situation where they find themselves either in danger or in desperate need.[20] Stress, on the other hand, can be either a physical, chemical, or emotional factor that causes bodily or mental tension. Ongoing stresses can cause various diseases.[21] As great as the inroads have been in today's medicine, our prescribed medications have not been able to find the root of our physical problems. Yes, they can relieve pain temporarily, but once they wear off the pain mysteriously returns.

What makes this discovery even more astounding is the fact that as I minister to people in the church, very rarely are the physical problems they are suffering from actually physical. Whether it is emotional or spiritual, I am finding out that praying a prayer for physical healing is not reaching the desired result. I find myself digging deeper into their lives, using words of knowledge to help me get to the root of the matter. Once that is found, if those who I am dealing will admit it to be true, we can then deal with the source and they will finally be set free to be healed.

When Jesus was condemned to die on the cross, we find that there were two other men who had been judged to die a similar death. Because of their sin, the judgment that was pronounced upon them was one of the most, if not the most, cruel and painful deaths a man could experience. According to the law of the land at that time, they were receiving exactly what they deserved. You could say then that their lives were in distress. I have always been awestruck by how two people in the same situation can react so differently. It has been said if you interview ten people after witnessing an accident, you will receive eleven different opinions. Even accepting that as true, it is still mind-boggling how we as people react so differently to similar situations.

### Two Different Reactions

The first criminal to voice his opinion was the one who made a statement in mocking fashion.

*Then one of the criminals who were hanged blasphemed Him, saying, "If You are the Christ, save Yourself and us."* (Luke 23:39)

The stresses and distresses we encounter in life will make us express words that are utter nonsense. The pain in our bodies and minds will have such a profound effect that we will say anything to escape this torture. Blaspheming the Lord was not below the dignity of this particular man, so railing, mocking, and ridiculing God was par for the course. We must not be so judgmental of this man, because Jesus Himself uttered some words under the pressure of sin that in reality were not true.

> *And about the ninth hour Jesus cried out with a loud voice, saying, "Eli, Eli, lama sabachthani?" that is, "My God, My God, why have You forsaken Me?"*
> (Matthew 27:46)

Taking that into consideration, examining the words of the other criminal being crucified becomes even more impressive. Whereas the words of his counterpart were filled with pride and arrogance, his words were laced with humility as he cried out one last time onto God. Before doing so, he had the wherewithal to put the other criminal in his place.

> *But the other, answering, rebuked him, saying, "Do you not even fear God, seeing you are under the same condemnation? And we indeed justly, for we receive the due reward of our deeds; but this Man has done nothing wrong." Then he said to Jesus, "Lord, remember me when You come into Your kingdom."*
> (Luke 23:40-42)

The Lord indeed had a response to both of their appeals. The arrogant, smug, scoffer went unnoticed and unheard, while the repentant criminal received a promise of eternal life.

> *And Jesus said to him, "Assuredly, I say to you, today you will be with Me in Paradise."*
> (Luke 23:43)

If there was ever a cry worth the trouble, it was that one.

## The Impact of Crying Out

The impact of crying out onto God was a way of communicating that the Lord Himself used. After the effects of crucifixion had taken its toll on His body physically, even under the severest of afflictions, He still found Himself reaching out to lost souls. Once His mission was complete, with distress written all over His face, He made one last ditch effort to cry out unto God. Although His breathing alone became a major effort, He garnered up enough strength for one final cry.

*Now it was about the sixth hour, and there was darkness over all the earth until the ninth hour. Then the sun was darkened, and the veil of the temple was torn in two. And when Jesus had cried out with a loud voice, He said, "Father, 'into Your hands I commit My spirit.'....* (Luke 23:44-46)

The apostle John took over recording his final words when he wrote this:

*...He said, "It is finished!" And bowing His head, He gave up His spirit.* (John 19:30)

What does this all mean to us as we attempt to live our lives for Him? When we cry out to the Lord with a loud voice in our distress, what we are in reality doing is imitating Him, following His example. This not only guarantees He will hear our cries, but is able to answer them as well. What is that answer? It is finished, it is already done. Your time of affliction will be nothing more than a bad memory in your past, as well. One whose bearing on your life will be whittled down to nothing over time. Restoration will not only bring you back to normalcy, it will then allow you to be exalted by God (1 Peter 5:6-7).

### It Was Worth It All

I would like to end this chapter once again talking about my mom. In previous chapters, I had made mention of the great influence she had helping me understand the importance of prayer. Like her mother before her, she used the time set aside to be alone with God to approach His throne and His Majesty, speaking in other tongues. The transformation of her personality was so extreme it was difficult to believe it was really her. She was not embarrassed to moan and groan in the spirit, and with her tears she was able to make headway in the spiritual realm like few others could. It was those tears that would move me as I would put my ear to the door, just like I did when I was a little boy hearing Grandma pray. I was much older now, yet what I heard penetrating through the door had the same effect. This is worth mentioning because it took an extremely long amount of time for my mom to have her prayers answered. It would be more than twenty years living as a single parent before she was to marry the man she lived with for the rest of her life. It was a time in society when divorce was unfavorably looked upon. Not only was she somewhat of an outcast in our local church, but the condescending behavior continued in the workplace as well.

There were periods of disenchantment, ones of disillusionment, but every day coming home from practice I would find her locked up in her room, crying out to her God. When the Lord finally did respond to her supplications, what He had provided was more than she could ever imagine. After marriage, although you could not consider her rich, she lived her life in want of nothing. She had the ability to travel on weekends with no reservations. I recall talking to her every once in a while on the phone on a Saturday afternoon, asking where she was. We lived in southern California at the time, and her itch to travel at times took her outside of the state. It was common for her to respond to my question with, "We are in Arizona or in Oklahoma," or other vacation spots that would be more than 100 miles away at least.

You could tell by her countenance she had been rejuvenated, and revived not only in spirit but physically as well. Her smile and laugh were effervescent and they certainly glistened perpetually. Her life had unquestionably taken a turn for the better, but it did come at a great cost. The times of doubts were many, interspersed with a few moments of faith. The tears at times would not stop and her mind would tire from all of the afflictions and stress. But if you had the opportunity today to speak to her about her life and if it was all worth it, I doubt very much if you would hear any pessimistic words come from her mouth. She knew when she cried out onto her God, He heard her voice from His temple and it was clear enough for Him to hear, understand the situation, and respond in due time. Her cries were worth it all!

# CHAPTER 9

## In the Palm of His Hands

*See, I have inscribed you on the palms of My hands;*
*Your walls are continually before Me.*

(Isaiah 49:16)

Engraved images are truly a work of art. The stories they tell are diverse, but usually they are of an artist who has taken his time to make sure this carved handiwork would be considered something sensational. The time and effort to produce such a masterpiece cannot be calculated in minutes or sweat. There are no time limits placed on these exquisite creations, because never would it enter into the mind of the artist to cheat himself of an opportunity to create something that few other people could. Perfection takes time, yet when an artist is truly engulfed in his work, it is easy to lose track of it. The end result then will be a fine, detailed, and precise stroke of genius to be admired by all.

### Impressed by Their Handiwork

I recall on a mission trip to Panama a couple of years ago how I was utterly impressed with the wood carvings of some tribes women we had ministered to. After the gospel was presented and we had an opportunity to pray with them, they then took some time to show us their handiwork. The men of the tribe had left earlier in the morning to work, leaving the women to care for the children. Being industrious as they were, they took it upon themselves to take up a craft that would bring in extra income to the family. As a group, they had chosen to try their hand at woodcarving. As they displayed to us the different animals they had carved out of wood, we were surprisingly stunned by these precise, intricate artifacts. The detail itself proved that the work created here was meticulous, methodically and carefully done.

Of course a price was set for each of the sculptures as they made their way to Panama City. On the other hand the work, at least in their eyes, was priceless. The value of any creation, whether carved, painted, or usually will depend on the creator himself. I could take a bunch of paint and splatter it onto a canvas, and my work of art would not be worth much. But, if my last name were to be Picasso, that same painting would be worth millions. That goes to show many times what is valued so highly in this world is dependent upon our knowledge of who created it in the first place.

### Our Value Comes from Him

Taking that into consideration, the Scriptures tell us that we, the children of God, have been inscribed or engraved in the palm of His hands. He started from scratch with nothing more than dirt and mud to work with. Even with these limited resources, He was able to create a masterpiece. His work of art was detailed, meticulously put together, and was particularly thorough. He wanted to make sure that this creation would mirror His image, so He took His time to create. This is where we get our worth. We are nothing without Him, and only because the King of glory has made us His creation, we are worth far more than we deserve.

Of all of the characteristics God placed in man, the fact that He gave him a will is somewhat baffling. This was baffling in the sense that mankind was created with a penchant and the ability to sin. That would prove disastrous in the future, meaning he would make bad decisions, err in judgment, and at times choose to rebel against his maker. In the same breath, the Lord gave us, His creation, an ability to love. This ability unique to man would allow him to worship God without being forced. Moreover, understanding he was not a puppet on a string, man could serve his God without the feeling of being a slave. The ultimate goal would be to cultivate a desire from man to love God the way God loved him.

Summing things up, we come to the conclusion that man will fail more than he will succeed, that goes without saying. There will be occasions that our lives are more of a reproach than a blessing, and we will embarrass Him more than bring Him pride. In God's foreknowledge, He already knew this. Although it has been said insanity is doing the same thing over and over again and expecting a different result (Albert Einstein)[22], God is the only one who can expect different results from us when we have continued to fail Him in the past without Him being insane. This is why His opinion about us has never changed.

*For He remembered that they were but flesh, a breath that passes away and does not come again.*
(Psalms 78:39)

Recognizing we are prone to failure, He has provided a failsafe way to keep us in good standing. It is His unmerited favor, otherwise known as grace.

*And He said to me, "My grace is sufficient for you, for My strength is made perfect in weakness." Therefore most gladly I will rather boast in my infirmities, that the power of Christ may rest upon me.* (2 Corinthians 12:9-10)

For those of you who believe you have stumbled so far away from God that even His grace cannot reach down and snatch you out of the enemy's grip, you are badly mistaken. It was for our transgressions that God was willing to pay the ultimate price, dying for us on the cross. It is when we have hit rock bottom with nothing of God inside of us that He does His best work. He chomps at the bit, so to say, to have another opportunity to use His strength when we are at our weakest. In the minds of those who don't know Him, it sounds like a plan that was destined to fail from the beginning. On the other hand, in our minds, as His children we are ever thankful that His grace is always available to swoop down wherever we may be to pick us up and save us.

### The Woman Without a Name

The Bible records a story that is somewhat odd in its presentation of this Bible character. Luke writes to us about a woman without a name (Luke 7:36-50). In actuality, she did have a name, but it was never mentioned because her reputation was such that there's no need to even articulate her name. She went by the label, "the woman who was a sinner." Now, have you ever entered into a conversation late where everybody else in that particular group has already started without you? Although they are not naming any names, as soon as you hear the details of what is going on, you know exactly who they are talking about. Isn't it amazing how we can recognize who people are even without ever mentioning their names? When your name has been tainted by a bad reputation, gaining it back is literally impossible. That is one reason why Scripture admonishes us to keep our good name (reputation) in good standing.

*A good name is to be chosen rather than great riches...* (Proverbs 22:1)

As far as this "woman who was a sinner" was concerned, we find out later in Scripture indirectly what the offense was to receive such a harsh label. The details of her life were few and we really don't know how she got started in this particular profession (prostitution). Was it her own choice or did something traumatic happen in her life to fall into this? From my experiences dealing with abused people, whether sexually, physically, or emotionally, it doesn't really matter, take your pick. I have found out that from these abuses, many times promiscuity arises. Is this what happened to this woman at an earlier age? We can only speculate because Scripture is mute regarding this subject. What we do know about her, by her actions, is this. She hated her present life, which she hid very well by her ostentatious lifestyle. She was good at what she did and she got paid well for it. The problem that arose was similar to the one addicted people have to face when dealing with any vice. They really want stop, but they just don't know how. In her mind, she was in way too deep to get out now, her bad decisions could not be reversed. The appearance and confidence she portrayed in public was nothing compared to the dismay she felt on the inside. She was literally falling apart, and there was nothing she could do about it.

For some time now, she had heard about a man in the area performing miracles, not only physical ones but emotional ones as well. As she bounced the idea in her head about confronting this man of God, her greatest fear was that of rejection. If there was anyone in the world who understood what rejection was all about, it was her. I mean, except for her lovers she had no friends. The other ladies in the city would not even give her the time of day. She was clothed in the best that money could buy, her perfumes shipped in from the Orient, with more money than she could ever possibly spend. The problem was the fact that she had nobody in her life she could enjoy it with, and that brought great depression.

### Standing Across the Street

How she got the nerve to stand across the street where Jesus was ministering that day, we do not know because Scripture does not mention it. I can only imagine what was going through her head and what she was trying to reconcile in her thoughts. What perhaps she had difficulty in accepting was, although she had chosen a lifestyle condemned by the Scriptures and of God, she still was a daughter of Jehovah. A child of God will never forfeit the benefits promised in the word, as long as there is a willing heart to repent of that wrong and walk in newness of life. Jeremiah pretty much confirmed this when he wrote this Scripture about the great love the Lord has for His people.

> *Then I will give them a heart to know Me, that I am the LORD; and they shall be My people, and I will be their God, for they shall return to Me with their whole heart.* (Jeremiah 24:7)

The best heaven had to offer was only a prayer away. With a concerted effort, restoration could be found with a humbled heart, which He would never turn away. In her mind, if any of this was going to work, the Lord would need to create a new heart in her because hers had been broken so many times. That, of course, was doable because she was dealing with the creator of the universe and He could create anything.

> *I form the light and create darkness, I make peace and create calamity; I, the LORD, do all these things.* (Isaiah 45:7)

The next step would be her most difficult one because it would be her first step towards the Master. It has been said the most difficult task to complete is the one that is never started. Whoever this statement is credited to, one must admit there's a lot of wisdom in those words. Look how Helen Keller expressed herself, talking about a similar situation:

"You have set yourselves a difficult task, but you will succeed if you persevere; and you will find joy in overcoming obstacles. Be of good cheer. Do not think of today's failures, but of the success that may come tomorrow... Remember, no effort that we make to attain something beautiful is ever lost."[23]

With a deep breath, she made her way to the other side of the street. She could hear the Master's words as He was delivering His message of hope, and it was almost enough to stop her in her tracks. But the determination that had brought her this far took over the situation and she opened the door, stepping inside. I can imagine the horrified looks and gasps directed her way as those who knew her could not believe her nerve to just barge in. For those in the crowd that day who did not recognize her, one look at the alabaster box caused their reaction to be the same. For a woman of ill repute, her alabaster box was one of her most prized possessions. The box itself was costly, but the perfumes inside even more so. It was the use of these perfumes that allowed her to seduce her lovers, creating a lifestyle of luxury that few people would ever attain. Outrage and anger were only two of the emotions displayed by the shocked crowd, but when Jesus discerned their indignation He quelled them with a parable. He asked Simon who would be more grateful when a debt was forgiven. Would it be the person forgiven of little or much? Of course, Simon answered, the one who had been forgiven much. Jesus then went on to confront the crowd directly, explaining to them what had just happened as this sinner woman gave her offering.

> *And He said to him, "You have rightly judged." Then He turned to the woman and said to Simon, "Do you see this woman? I entered your house; you gave Me no water for My feet, but she has washed My feet with her tears and wiped them with the hair of her head. You gave Me no kiss, but this woman has not ceased to kiss My feet since the time I came in. You did not anoint My head with oil, but this woman has anointed My feet with fragrant oil. Therefore I say to you, her sins, which are many, are forgiven, for she loved much. But to whom little is forgiven, the same*

loves little." Then He said to her, "Your sins are forgiven." (Luke 7:43-48)

## A Foregone Conclusion?

The fact that Jesus received her offering unquestionably does not prove that it was a foregone conclusion. Notice from the Scripture that as she initially approached Him, it was from behind (Luke 7:38), indicating there was still some doubt as to whether she would be accepted or not. Her great show of emotion as she wiped His feet with her tears was more than enough evidence to God that she could be forgiven. After the rebuke of the crowd, He said something that I found profound. Look at verse 50 of Luke chapter 7: *Then He said to the woman, "Your faith has saved you. Go in peace."* I found this statement profound in that the story written by Luke, in my opinion, is more of a demonstration of love than faith. Disagree with me if you will, but as I picture this woman completely broken before the Lord, anointing His feet with her most prized possession, that just shouts out to me, "unabashed love" being demonstrated by her. Because the Lord is not a man that He should lie, there has to be an answer even if it's not logical. As I dug a little bit deeper, I found where Jesus was coming from, and my understanding was opened. It indeed was faith demonstrated by her that day that brought her freedom. But the faith Jesus saw in her was not initiated at the time of the washing of His feet. He realized it was faith that originated and released in her crossing of the street. She had no guarantees, assurances, or a single promise that she would be forgiven, much less allowed to minister unto Him. Yet, by faith she took that first step. It turned out to be a step that would change the course of her life.

The testimony you have just read in Scripture is one of the many descriptive examples the Lord leaves for us in His word. He has chosen this method of communication not only to boost our faith, but because in His wisdom He understands that we relate to picture words as well. Pictures help us to explain the unexplainable, those situations in life that do not make any sense whatsoever. I had chosen the Scripture in Isaiah 49 that was used at the beginning of the chapter to help demonstrate this fact. The first part of the Scripture is self-explanatory; it took me a little more research to figure out where the Lord was going when He allowed Isaiah to use those picture words.

## Using Picture Words to Communicate

There's not much left to the imagination when you read that God has us inscribed in the palm of His hand. It was important for God to use Isaiah's writings to help us, as His children, to comprehend in a more illustrative manner how He would never leave us nor forsake us (Hebrews 13:5). There are at least two occurrences I can think of in our own experiences that help us understand the points God is trying to make for us. First of all, have you ever had a cut in the palm of your hand? It could be as non-threatening as a paper cut, or one deep enough for some type of surgical repair. Be what it may, contact with any object will be proof positive that your cut is still there. Until it actually heals completely, every bumping of the hand will cause some kind of pain in your body. Second of all, in the days that we are living in (2013), tattoos are exceptionally popular. It has gone to the extreme that the tattoos are considered body art. That being said, until technology catches up, to get rid of a tattoo is easier said than done. The Lord through Isaiah wanted us to know that the covenant He had made with us is a long-lasting one. He is not a fly-by-night kind of God, one who is here today and gone tomorrow. We can count on Him every hour of the day, every day of the week, every week of the month, and every month of the year. We will find out that to rid ourselves of Him will not be very easy. Adding to this example of tattoos, we must consider the exact spot where God has placed them. Would it not be more logical to have placed our image on His arm or shoulder? Perhaps, but because His hands are hands of provision, every time He extends those hands to provide for someone else, our image is right in front of His eyes. What a wonderful reminder to Him that our petition still has not been answered and still needs to be dealt with. Even for some crazy reason He would want to get rid of us, we are etched in the palm of His hand, not easily to be forgotten. If you can picture that through this Scripture, then the Lord has accomplished His goal through the words of Isaiah.

### *A Picture Not Easily Understood*

The second portion of the Scripture is not as easily descriptive. This illustration needs some explanation and it took me some time to figure out its importance. *Your walls are continually before me* just did not trigger any spiritual benefits to me until I began to consider walls in everyday life and their uses by us. For some reason, I started with the walls inside of a home and I began to picture them in every area of the house. In the construction of many homes, once you open the front door you are led into the rest of the house through a hallway. More times than not, in that hallway, you will find pictures. These pictures span the history of that particular family, usually from day one. On that wall you will find wedding day pictures, pictures of babies' births, and everything in between, including graduations of different times in their education. Through those pictures, you will find that at one time the bride was only a size four, as well as the fact that in those days the husband was not bald. You'll see the various growth spurts of each child, and perhaps even gaze upon someone on the wall you do not recognize. Not knowing there has been a death of a child in the family, you inquire who this is and why aren't there more pictures of them? This will bring an answer to your question, but one that is given with reservation and grief written all over it. All in all, the pictures on the wall tell stories of good times and bad times as well.

I believe the Lord helped Isaiah use these picture words again to help us to understand God's commitment to us throughout our lifetime. That is something we can build upon to strengthen our relationship with the Lord. On the other hand, with our experiences both good and bad right before Him, He can freely walk the hallways and corridors of heaven with constant reminders that there is still work to be done in our lives.

These same walls used to hang our most precious memories are also the ones that have tumbled, and been toppled during tumultuous times. They continue to tell the stories of dreams never coming to pass, or desires abandoned because of sin. They have been shaken by plans gone awry, relationships gone bad and bad health cutting lives short. As Nehemiah stood before the broken walls of Jerusalem with a burden for his people, so does the Lord stand before our broken walls with the greatest of desires to reconstruct our lives to a place of peace.

With all of the pictures, illustrations, and metaphors used by the Lord to convince us His mercy is great enough to restore our lives completely, the doubts built up over this extended time of affliction make it all very difficult to believe. Why so? Because it has the appearance of something easy, and as the old adage says, if it's too good to be true then it's not![24] That might be true in any other case, but as far as the word of God is concerned it does not hold water.

### Paint Him a Picture

What are we to do then, when in the past our words and our pleadings were not good enough to register an answer from the Almighty? It is as simple as painting a picture. When you don't know what to say, when discouragement has come because of a lack of words, paint a picture of your emotions similar to that of the "woman who was a sinner." Her actions not only spoke louder than her words would have, but there is another saying that no one seems to take credit for, which could also have come into play. "A picture is worth 1,000 words."[25] Without an utterance, this woman began to paint a masterpiece of a picture. It was one that not only moved the Lord to forgive her, but a picture to be admired for coming generations.

I believe we can apply those same actions to our lives today with similar results. You may not know what to say, how to say it, or if it is the right time or not, but you can take courage in the fact that this woman felt the same way. It begins at the altar of humility. Don't be afraid to paint a picture of sheer futility, because if you do it in faith, it is the best picture you will ever paint. It will also confirm to Him that you believe you have been placed in the palm of His hands, a place where God does His best work.

# CHAPTER 10

## Nevertheless God Will Make a Way

*Behold, I will do a new thing, now it shall spring forth shall you not know it? I will even make a road in the wilderness and rivers in the desert.*
(Isaiah 43:19)

Nevertheless has always been an intriguing word to me. In actuality, it is three words put together to form one. If we take those words separately, two of them are somewhat ineffectual. A life filled with "never" could not possibly be a life worth pursuing. It is even worse to have the label of always doing the "least" attached to any of our efforts. Finally, the word "the" has no meaning at all, and who would want to chase dreams that land up being meaningless? We can actually put those three words together as one phrase and get a completely different description. The phrase, "never the less," does not put a guarantee on obtaining the best (our assumption), but what is produced will not be the least.

We can then take the word standing alone and its definition becomes weightier. By definition, "nevertheless" means in spite of.[26] Regardless of our afflictions, frailties, shortcomings, insecurities, doubts, and failures, He, our God, still offers us His best. There are sixty-four more mentions of this word in the Old Testament, but only in this occasion does it speak with such sovereignty mixed with hope. The Hebrew word used here, **yasha`**, means God will avenge, defend, preserve, rescue, and bring salvation to those who trust Him.[27]

There is even a hidden "oneness" message we can extrapolate to strengthen our position in understanding the revelation of the Godhead. No one in their right mind would ever admit to serving three separate persons, but the Trinitarian doctrine is willing to put three separate persons in one Godhead.[28] This is very much like making the three separate words never, the, and less into one phrase that makes more sense, making it more monotheistic. It is only when we put God as one word and not a phrase, moving through eternity manifesting Himself in different ways that we get the full impact of His power and glory.

### *Being creative*

The Scripture we cited in Isaiah says that God will do a new thing, and to do a new thing, some type of creating must take place. Being creative is nothing more than to bring something into existence through imaginative skill or design.[29] You would think that with the study of the human body being so accessible to anyone in the world today, common sense would tell you that the human body is not the happenstance of an unintended explosion. The designer of its complex systems, at the very least, would have to be a genius with more going for him than a "Big

Bang theory," making it even more difficult to accept the theory of evolution. Take some time to truly examine the respiratory and circulatory systems. You cannot disregard or overlook the nervous and reproductive systems as well.

Just the fact medicine itself cannot generalize its methods and medications to treat all of these systems the same for our recovery should tell us something. Every single one of these areas has become specialized, and even then doctors are still learning about their particular discipline. There is no such thing as an expert in these areas because there is far more to learn than the amount they know, hence a continual process of learning carries on. If we can accept the fact that God with His unlimited imagination was responsible for our creation, then we can easily admit the creation of man truly accentuates His creativity. Add to this the realization that He created us from nothing, and you have a rock solid argument for the creative powers of our God.

### The Dark Side of Creativity

If only all creativity was as constructive as the creativity of our God. Sad to say, the creative juices flowing through the wicked mind are far more potent in creating devastation that is difficult to recover from. That usually is the underlying purpose of creative accounting. Unusual accounting practices are performed with the intention of deceiving management, and if they are successful they incur losses to companies that never saw it coming. That is exactly how satan works in a Christian's life. He deceptively creates illusions to conceal the truth, defraud us of true peace, and his elaborate scheme develops into nothing more than a fantasy.

On the other hand, when God creates, He creates in perfection.

> *I have made the earth, and created man on it. I — My hands — stretched out the heavens, and all their host I have commanded. I have raised him up in righteousness, and I will direct all his ways;*
> (Isaiah 45:12-13)

What a promise He has left to us in that after being created so perfectly, the care of our God continues in lifting us up in righteousness. If that is not enough, whenever the need arises He will direct us in all our ways. For years the Coca-Cola Bottling Company made millions of dollars on its motto, "It's the Real Thing." It is a model that should have been attributed to our God's ability to create, because He truly has created the real thing. There are no illusions, it is not temporary, and God knows it will not self-destruct.

The only responsibility given to humanity is to express appreciation for the fact God has created us, by giving Him daily praise.

> *This will be written for the generation to come, that a people yet to be created may praise the LORD.*
> (Psalms 102:18)

### When Obstacles Get in the Way

Being created in His image, in total perfection, should be enough in our lives to keep us on the straight and narrow. However, the enemy's fiery darts play a big part in hindering our receiving God's best. The occasional obstacle course we must maneuver through is difficult enough to slow down our progress in God's kingdom. An obstacle can be someone or something that interferes with or slows down the progress of something in our lives.[30] Like afflictions defined in past chapters, obstacles were meant to be temporary, and only temporary. The enemy's main function then is to try to convince us that they really are permanent. The longer they linger in our lives, creating mayhem, the easier it becomes to believe. The similarities of obstacles and afflictions bear such a striking resemblance that sometimes it's hard to tell the difference. Again, like afflictions, obstacles come in various forms. They can be physical or mental, and even extend out to financial problems.

When trying to find relief, it is so disheartening to hear the so-called experts counseling us that in their expert opinion there is really no hope for us. Because satan continues to aggravate our lives in ways that are not known to man, many times they don't even have a single word of advice to help relieve our pain. The Lord, on the other hand, has a different viewpoint. Look at His response to the hopeless situations in our lives.

> *Behold, I will do a new thing, now it shall spring forth; shall you not know it? I will even make a road in the wilderness and rivers in the desert.*
> (Isaiah 43:19)

If God has to pull a rabbit out of His hat, so to speak, that is possible. Even though it may be, He would never choose to go that route because most people would consider that magic or a hoax. Those means of taking care of business are usually reserved for witches and the occult. When God provides, it is not an illusion or sleight of hand, it's the real thing. If He has to go to a place in His arsenal that has never been used before, and is unknown to man, again He is not limited in any way, shape, or form. All we need to do is put it in His hands and watch the Master work.

### Trusting God to Do a New Thing

Trusting Him when He does a new thing in our lives is always an adventure, because we really never know which way He is going to provide. It may be something new to us, but we must come to the realization that it's not new to Him. As far as miracles go, He has been creating them from the time He created the world itself. We are the ones who need to catch up to Him and His glory so we can, without any hesitation, let God be God. Because we are His children, there is an abundant amount of promises at our disposal. One of these promises found in the Psalms allows us to unconditionally trust in Him.

> *And those who know Your name will put their trust in You; for You, LORD, have not forsaken those who seek You.* (Psalms 9:10)

The fact that we know His name, and who He is, brings about benefits not known to the rest of this world. There is power in the name of Jesus, and once a child of God understands what has been placed in his hands, he can release that power to see the glory of God manifested in miraculous ways. His name has been revealed to us for a purpose and that purpose is to allow the fullness of God the liberty to work unhindered in a world where most people do not know Him.

If knowing His name were the only requirement to live a successful life in God, more people would be doing great and mighty things for Him in their lives. A person wise enough to understand that the name of the one true God has been revealed to them will take that next step to draw closer to Him.

*But it is good for me to draw near to God; I have put my trust in the Lord GOD, that I may declare all Your works.* (Psalms 73:28)

Drawing close to God is a prerequisite to trusting Him for the impossible because there'll be times situations will arise when one must embark in unfamiliar territory. We cannot fear the unknown when we are in places that take us out of our comfort zone. It is in that place of uncharted waters that the Lord will go out of His way to reveal His secrets to us. Knowing that few of His children will venture out in places that others won't dare to go, He relishes the time one will sacrifice to be alone with Him.

### A More Surprising Revelation

Because trust is a two-way street and is very much reciprocal at the height of its effectiveness, there are times the Lord will go out on a limb, extending His trust to those who do not know Him as their personal Savior.

*When you cry out, let your collection of idols deliver you. but the wind will carry them all away, a breath will take them. But he who puts his trust in Me shall possess the land, and shall inherit My holy mountain."* (Isaiah 57:13)

A pastor friend of mine told me this testimony recently that proves this to be true. There was a particular couple he had tried to evangelize over a period of years. Every once in a while, after losing contact he would find them again, and immediately renew his efforts to present them the gospel. Because life had been good to the husband, owning a prosperous business, serving God was not one of his greatest priorities. Very much like the Laodicean church, he was in need of nothing. Unlike the Laodicean church, he did not know Jesus as his personal Savior. No matter how he presented the gospel to his old friend, the pastor never was able to get a commitment from either of them. My pastor friend understood unless something drastic happened, it would always be this way. After losing track of him the last time, it somewhat eased the burden and their lives once again were put on the back burner.

Once again they bumped into each other, and as the pastor began to pray for this couple with renewed interest, the Lord spoke to him and said, "Give your friend a call and tell him there is a family member that is deathly sick. You have been instructed by me (God) to go and pray for that family member, and if allowed to do so, I (God) will heal them." As the pastor dialed his friend's number, little did he know the daughter was suffering from pancreatitis. Although the daughter had been prayed for by others before that, the healing she received was only good enough to avoid death. The disease was still running its course and needed to be healed completely. The friend was astounded by the pastor's knowledge of something that had kept him on pins and needles for seven years. After the prayer was allowed, she no longer returned to the hospital for procedures that kept her bedridden for a week at a time on a monthly basis. With the pain subsiding with each and every day, she has been able to reduce her dosage of pain medication almost to nothing.

The most interesting bit of information I had gathered from her in our conversation was what the doctor told her when she asked a pointed question. "Will I ever be a normal person again?" She asked inquisitively. As intelligent as he wanted to appear, this is the only answer he could come up with. "I really don't know, because no one I have treated in the past in your condition has lived as long as you, they're usually dead after seventy-two hours," he admitted sheepishly. Can you imagine that! A doctor who was considered an expert in his field had no clue as to what was going on in the body of his patient. I can tell you exactly what was going on with her. God was doing a new thing, something that only He could produce, and something that could not be duplicated by any doctor in the world.

This show of mercy fell upon a family that really didn't know God. In the past, in their pursuit of happiness, they could always count on their collection of idols (not literally) to help them along the way. By idols I mean someone or something other than God that they trusted completely. But when a situation arose where the obstacle before them became unsolvable and the affliction became too severe, those in whom they had placed their confidence in the past were driven away by the wind. In other words, at the first sign of calamity, they were nowhere to be found. On the other hand, for the very first time, without really knowing how to pray, they called on the name of Jesus and He responded.

His response to them was similar to His response to all His children. They had opened up the doors to His provision, and boy, does God know how to provide. For the first time in their lives, they possessed the land and were inheriting God's holy mountain meaning "They shall enjoy the privileges of the church on earth, and be brought at length to the joys of heaven; and no wind shall carry them away."[31] It was at this time all three received the baptism of the Holy Ghost, speaking in other tongues. Mom and dad went one step further in giving their lives completely unto God by being baptized in the name of Jesus for the forgiveness of their sins.

### It Doesn't Take Much to Produce a Miracle

Because they were willing to blindly cry out on to a God unknown to them, putting their trust in Him, they came away with a miracle many said was impossible. The God we serve is not only all-powerful but ever willing to show His power and mercy. If that is so, and it is, then why are there not more miracles performed in this world? There has been too much focus on the afflictions of life without ever considering the one who has the power to take them away. In other words, it takes a childlike faith to believe God will go out of His way to create a miracle beyond belief.

I am completely convinced that most people have the faith necessary to receive the solution only God can provide. We all basically believe God can do anything. It's that trickle of unbelief that He can do it in our behalf that stops Him in His tracks.

> *Jesus said to him, "If you can believe, all things are possible to him who believes." Immediately the father of the child cried out and said with tears, "Lord, I believe; help my unbelief!"* (Mark 9:23-24)

It is so easy to identify with this father who had approached Jesus with a prayer request that His disciples could not answer. At the end of his rope, he broke down in tears before the Master. The combination of the seizures his boy suffered from and the constant care needed to keep him from killing himself finally had taken its toll emotionally. For all that he had suffered over such a long period of time, he was confident that he could muster up enough faith to receive his miracle. The problem arose when doubts of unbelief began to torment him as violently as the seizures tormented his son. It is one thing to believe

God for great things. It is another thing to believe God for great things in your own life. Have you ever felt that way? You know God can do anything, but is He willing to go to that extreme for you? The only way you will be able to find out is to step out by faith and put it to work. Faith without works is dead (James 2:26). At the admission of his spiritual inadequacies, the Lord provided a miracle anyway and casted out the dumb spirit from his son. I think a popular saying would be appropriate to place in his situation, to prove that all of us are not very far from our miracle. "Said and done."

### *Case in Point*

When traveling through the Midwest at the end of last year, we spent quite a bit of time in the state of Indiana. In a particular church where we were ministering for the first time, I really wasn't sure what to expect. During the preliminaries, a great spirit of worship could be felt throughout the entire church. It is usually during those times I will briefly survey the congregation and see if there's anything the Lord would like me to pay attention to in my preaching or ministering in the spirit. That morning, my gaze fell upon a couple who appeared out of place. I say out of place because their way of dress was distinctively from the 70s. I thought the days of the hippie and its culture had been long gone. I guess not. As simple as their dress was, I wondered if their way of thinking would also be along those lines. I say that because people who are not complicated in any way have the ability to believe God for great things.

When it came time to minister to the sick, the wife hobbled to the altar with her prayer request. She made it known she had suffered from scoliosis (a lateral curvature of the spine) for many years. On top of that, her right leg was about three inches shorter than the left, thus the hobbling as she walked. Finally, her right arm was somewhat stiff and her movements were restricted. Although she was an adult now for some years, the look on her face told another story. She gazed into my eyes the way a little girl would, with all the hope in the world at her disposal. When I asked her if she believed God could heal her, she responded with a resounding yes. After a simple prayer, the pain in her back immediately left and there was some extended movement in the arm. As I had her walk to see if anything had happened with her leg, she continued to hobble. I then sat her down, lifting her leg toward me, and prayed again. This time when she got up to walk, she walked perfectly. The creator of the universe had extended His hand of mercy upon her and did a new thing, a thing that up to that point she never knew was possible. It really did not take much on her part to be the recipient of God's best. That's the way it should be in all of our lives, constantly receiving the best God has to offer, bringing us to a place of peace.

## Why We Don't See More Miracles Today

Our answer is found in the passage of Scripture presented at the beginning of this chapter. If we study the spiritual condition of Israel at the time Isaiah wrote, we find that they were in utter despair. Captivity to the Babylonians had taken its toll and their morale was at its lowest. Faith amongst them was pretty much nonexistent because they had lived in defeat way too long. Taking that into consideration, the Lord had Isaiah admonish the people in the same chapter as a reminder to them who He really was.

*I am the LORD, your Holy One, the Creator of Israel, your King."* (Isa 43:15)

## Nevertheless, God Will Make a Way

For Israel to remember that their God, Jehovah, was their Holy King and Savior was a no-brainer. They had countless memories of all that during their exodus from Egypt, and it was forever ingrained in their minds. Sad to say, with the passage of time their image of God as a creator had fallen by the wayside. If God was to break them out from captivity, it was needful for them to believe that He could create a miracle on their behalf.

The church of today rejoices in the fact that they have found a King and Savior who has provided for them a new life in God. What most of us in the church today don't realize is that the God we serve continues to hold the title as Creator. We should not settle for less in God's provision for us because salvation is only the first step. His promises and blessings to us extend to our everyday lives as well and should be taken advantage of. We need to take the instructions given to Israel and apply them to our own lives.

*Forget the former things; do not dwell on the past.*
*(Isaiah 43:18 NIV)*

In spite of your past, nevertheless, put your failures behind you. Forget the times you weren't healed and the times the stresses of life had overwhelmed you. Erase, if you will, the relationships gone bad in times past and the financial difficulties that handcuffed your prosperity. Nevertheless, in spite of it all, God is waiting for an opportunity to create a new thing in your life. He is a master in creation and is the only God who can create masterpieces from nothing. Afflictions aside, let Him create for you today!

# End Notes

[1] Prophets and Personal Prophecy, Bill Hamon, pg. 35
[2] Merriam-Webster.com/dictionary/affliction
[3] Nelsons Bible dictionary/affliction
[4] International Standard Bible Encyclopedia/Leah
[5] Army.mil/info/organization/unitsandcommands/command structure/theoldguard/specplt/tomb.htm
[6] Ibid.
[7] New Unger's Bible dictionary/Jochebed
[8] En.Wikipedia.org/wiki/ Marilyn Munster
[9] Strong's Concordance (OT: 6961)
[10] www.merriam-webster.com/seek
[11] wiki answers.com, famous people, Benjamin Franklin
[12] wiki.answers.com ›... › Categories › Religion & Spirituality › Judaism
[13] ibid.
[14] en.wikipedia.org/wiki/Wall_of_Jericho
[15] Merriam-Webster.com/dictionary/tender
[16] ibid.
[17] ibid.
[18] Strong's Hebrew – Greek dictionary (OT 5048)
[19] Merriam-Webster.com/dictionary/cry
[20] Merriam-Webster.com/dictionary/distress
[21] Merriam-Webster.com/dictionary/stress
[22] brainyquote.com/quotes/quotes/a/alberteins
[23] inspirationpeak.com/cgi-bin/search.cgi?search=Helen+Keller
[24] Oxfordreference.com/search?siteToSearch=if+something+is+too+good+to+be+true
[25] Wiki.answers.com/Q/Who_made_up_a_picture_is_worth_1000_words
[26] Merriam-Webster.com/dictionary/nevertheless

[27] Strong's Greek/Hebrew dictionary/nevertheless (OT: 3467)
[28] When originally writing this part of the chapter, I immediately received an error message from Microsoft Word. It stated my numbers agreement was wrong. Even English grammatical rules have a hard time figuring out the Trinitarian doctrine.
[29] Merriam-Webster.com/dictionary/create
[30] Merriam-Webster.com/dictionary/obstacle
[31] Matthew Henry's Commentary on the Whole Bible: New Modern Edition, Electronic Database.

# George Pantages Ministries

## BOOKS AVAILABLE IN ENGLISH

## LIBROS DISPONIBLES EN ESPAÑOL

**GEORGE PANTAGES**
Cell 512-785-6324
GEOPANJR@YAHOO.COM
GEORGEPANTAGES.COM

www.ingramcontent.com/pod-product-compliance
Lightning Source LLC
LaVergne TN
LVHW051605070426
835507LV00021B/2778